The Innocent and the Beautiful

A true story of love, death, and survival

Alan Atkinson

The Innocent and the Beautiful

Published by The Conrad Press Ltd. in the United Kingdom 2023

Tel: +44(0)1227 472 874

www.theconradpress.com

info@theconradpress.com

ISBN 978-1-915494-36-8

This work depicts actual events in the life of the author as truthfully as recollection permits.

Typesetting and Cover Design by: Charlotte Mouncey, www.bookstyle.co.uk

The Conrad Press logo was designed by Maria Priestley.

Printed and bound in Great Britain by Clays Ltd, Elcograf S.p.A.

The innocent and the beautiful
Have no enemy but time

William Butler Yeats

Contents

[Author's note: the title of this book, and the incidental quotations, are from 'In Memory of Eva Gore-Booth and Con Markiewicz' by W.B. Yeats, from *The Winding Stair and other poems* (1933)]

Preface

Dear shadows now you know it all

Tuesday 17 February 1981: the last of our five lovely blue-sky days in Sarasota Florida that we had squeezed into the children's half-term holiday. We were there on a whim, to celebrate buying our new house, our imminent move from Scotland to the south of England and the next big step in our lives together.

Excited and happy, my eleven-year-old son Nigel and his younger twin sisters Anna-Jane and Lucy-Claire managed a last-minute swim before it was time to set off for Miami Airport and the late-night British Airways flight back to London.

The evening was calm and clear, with little traffic, as we headed south in our red Mercury sedan. The bright lights of Fort Myers persuaded us to break the journey and enjoy the exuberance of Denny's, my daughters' favourite larger-than-life American diner. For all of us, a grand finale to our five-day treat.

My wife, Adrienne, remembered she had postcards to send and scurried to the blue post box, laughing as she said that we'd be home weeks before the cards arrived. After carefully settling the children into the back seat of our two-door car, she strapped herself in beside me, pointing out the large round moon which was now dominating the night sky.

The air was still warm and as the car moved smoothly and quietly along the straight unlit highway, I soon sensed that everybody was asleep.

With the darkness broken only by occasional headlights, the huge full moon was now my friend, outlining the sparse tall trees to my left. And what I thought might be water beyond.

Part one

Blossom from the summer's wreath.
Great windows open to the south

1

It was unusual to hire a video camera in 1980: they were hefty, awkward things. Video camera rental shops were rare and the nearest from our home in Helensburgh Dunbartonshire was in Ayrshire, near Prestwick Airport. As the crow flew, it was just across the Gare Loch, but for me in my old blue Saab it was a drive of about forty miles, needing to first go eastwards to cross the River Clyde over the new Erskine Bridge.

I made all that effort because I was on a mission. Gala night was coming up at Helensburgh Swimming Club, and Nigel, my eleven-year-old son and my hero in life was competing in the backstroke, crawl, and butterfly events. He was bound to win, he always did; but this time it would all be recorded for posterity.

Carrying the heavy camera, on gala night I was in our usual pole position next to the pool, alongside Adrienne, my slightly embarrassed wife – we'd been married for fifteen years - and Anna-Jane and Lucy-Claire. They were the most enthusiastic of all, cheering every time they saw Nigel's face, or even just an arm.

We were a happy and expectant band of four, and I was about to record it all. I'd quickly skimmed over the complicated camera instructions but felt ready to produce a BBC-quality documentary. I think the people behind us expected something on the television news later that evening.

I pressed the start button, warning lights flashed, I obviously hadn't read that part of the manual. The swimmers were in the pool about to start, and it was too dark to read the small print, so, blaming 'light problems' to the people behind us, I put the camera away and watched the gala like everybody else. Nigel, I'm sure, was relieved that his doting father with a big black box on his shoulder wasn't recording his every move. After perhaps my fleeting thought of throwing the camera into the pool, Adrienne, always sensible and calm, suggested we keep it for another week, so that I could read the instructions properly, but also record our family and the wonderful town we lived in. We might not be there much longer, because the For Sale notice had just gone up outside Firlands, our house in Upper Colquhoun Street. With what was to follow, I was very grateful for the six hours of film I did record.

Our projected move from Helensburgh in Dunbartonshire to Steyning in West Sussex, had been much debated, because we all loved Helensburgh. Absolutely everything, from the children's little primary school to the majestic scenery of Glen Fruin, where we walked and took picnics. We could walk down tree-lined roads to the Gare Loch or take a ten-minute drive to Loch Lomond. From the twin's bedroom on a clear day, you could make out the Isle of Arran.

Adrienne and the children especially had made lots of close friends, and the children's birthdays were always much anticipated, big happy events in April and October. So, 'Why move?', was the question, asked by Adrienne especially.

Looking back I wish we had stayed exactly where we were. For seven years I had been a pilot with British Airways, based at Glasgow Airport and flying the old propellered Vickers Viscount, mostly around the Highlands and Islands of

Scotland. The plane was old but still enjoyed by both passengers and crews, not least because of its big windows and reliability. In places like Shetland a plane was the only quick way to the mainland, and with those windows on a clear day you could see all the beauty that Scotland had to offer.

Early mornings often brought the best of the weather with calm winds, and the clean air of the Islands and Highlands brought almost endless visibility. That encouraged us to fly low, ostensibly to please the passengers because of those big windows, but sometimes seeing the sick bags collected afterwards made me wonder.

Early on a summer's morning we'd often creep low over the inlets of the west coast, waggling the wings over a crew peacefully having breakfast on an anchored sailing boat below. The weather further north in Orkney and Shetland wasn't often like that, but the splendour of the Western Isles made up for the cold winds of Shetland in winter and the rains of Caithness at just about any time of year.

Contrasts were the lure of Scotland for me. The highlight of it all was a beautiful calm summer day, when I flew in the Viscount to Orkney with my ten-year-old son Nigel sitting in the cockpit behind me. In our hour on the ground, we watched the puffins from the towering clifftops. He sat in the pilot's seat for a photograph, and the look of complete happiness on his face made my day, then as it does now.

My daughters, though twins, were very different. Lucy-Claire was very much a clone of her mother, even to the curly blonde hair. She could easily put her thoughts into words and kept us all amused with an easy confidence. A confidence that I think came partly in having a twin sister. I remember when Anna had a cold and wasn't going to school, hearing Lucy getting ready, 'I'm sure I'll be all right'. They looked to each other and got on well, looking up to their big brother as he looked after them. Anna-Jane and I had a very special link; one glance at me with her beautiful blue eyes and I knew what she was thinking. More diffident with an already inbuilt sense of style, she was always the first to reach out for our hands. Anna-Jane was the last member of my family that I touched, holding her hand to cross the road in Florida.

The Atkinsons began the eighties as a very happy family of six, with Sophie our King Charles Cavalier always affectionately part of the scene. Our house was up for sale, we had found a wonderful house to buy and we had decided to move. But only because we wanted to be together, and I was now flying Boeing 737s out of Gatwick Airport, five hundred miles to the south.

2

Adrienne was my first and perhaps only real love. Tall and attractive, she had inbuilt mothering skills which, allied to down to earth Yorkshire common sense, made her a good mother and a natural teacher of young children, as well as the perfect wife. She grew up in an extended family of teachers in Sheffield, so it was no surprise that she became one; not long after she started her three-year teacher training course at Alnwick Castle in Northumberland, I began my one-year training to be a pilot at the nearby Royal Air Force station Acklington.

In the spring of 1963, and a month after my twentieth birthday, I was fulfilling my dream of becoming an RAF pilot. It was a dream that had begun on the crossbar of my eldest brother's bike, taken to watch the planes at nearby RAF West Malling Airfield in Kent. Our ride to the airfield through the North Pole Woods always included a stop at the old cider house amongst the trees; it was a cider for John and a lemonade for me.

After watching the Meteor and Vampire jets at the airfield we went home, usually not stopping at the cider house, but always with me dreaming of those planes. Ten years later I was an eager volunteer to join my school's cadet force, and when just over the minimum age I flew three terrifying (though nobody knew how frightened I was) solo circuits in a glider. I wanted to be a pilot and got more than enough 'O' and 'A' Levels but lacked the confidence to even apply. I slipped into the idea of being an electrical engineer, then changed at the last moment to becoming an aeronautical engineer, the nearest career, I thought, to actually being a pilot. I joined the de Havilland Aircraft Company at Hatfield, beginning a five-year sandwich course, two years at Hatfield 'sandwiching' three years at Southampton University. It was interesting, and I worked (I use the term very loosely, I mostly watched) on 'Puffin': de Havilland's attempt to build a man-powered aircraft to win the £10,000 Kramer Prize. Top athletes and cyclists sat in Puffin's seat and pedalled like mad, but though it got airborne it couldn't stay aloft and turn at the same time, so the prize was lost.

At Hatfield, surrounded by many ex-RAF people, I began to think seriously about applying to become a pilot in the RAF. One night in my bed and breakfast room, I went to sleep after reading a magazine called *Royal Air Force Flying Review*. On the back was an advertisement headed, *Join the Air Force, see the world. Earn £5,000 a year at 25*. Next morning those words were staring at me, and by that evening I'd applied to see the world.

An initial interview followed by selection tests at Biggin Hill led to the life-changing letter inviting me to become an officer and a pilot in the RAF. I replied almost by return of post, resigned from my engineering course, and on 19 December 1962, became Officer Cadet 4231761 in the Royal Air Force.

After an Outward Bound course and three months of marching, with the odd instruction on how to become an officer, I arrived at 6 Flying Training School, RAF Acklington in Northumberland, ready to fly the Jet Provost, a single engine two-seat training plane. It was an exciting time.

Everything was structured and labelled in the RAF; my first

flight in the Jet Provost, on 15 July 1963, was labelled, 'Exercise One; Familiarisation'. I walked across the tarmac towards the plane in my brand new blue flying suit, with my white leather gloves and 'bone-dome' helmet under my arm. I noticed my instructor beside me had a banana in his hand. Perhaps it was part of familiarisation, and we'd have a picnic in the air. I didn't know that Flt Lt Stack Butterley was a legend for both his flying skills and his sense of humour. Stack flew us to 10,000 feet, then ate his banana. He then wound back the canopy, turned the plane upside down, and dropped the banana skin down to the void below. As I hung in my straps and looked down 10,000 ft, I didn't appreciate the joke. Nor I suppose did the person below us with a frozen banana skin on his head, though I think we were over water.

Stack's methods worked, and on 7 August after another flight with him, (Exercise 13), this time from RAF Ouston, the back-up airfield for Acklington, he got out the cockpit, slapped me on the shoulder and said, 'Right, you're on your own', and I was sent off for my first solo flight. Just a tense five-minute flight around the airfield, but a milestone.

Then it was a question of working through an exercise, first with an instructor and then repeated solo. Navigation was never my strong point, in the air or on the ground, but when airborne from Acklington it was almost impossible to get lost. You just flew eastwards till you reached the coast, then north or south, (deciding which, was the tricky bit), until you came to the River Amble, and the airfield never moved from being just inland from there.

I was now Acting Pilot-Officer Atkinson. We were called 'General Duties Officers', meaning that we were RAF officers first, and pilots second. Various formal and less formal occasions were set up as part of our training, with an appropriate uniform for each occasion. One was a cocktail lounge scenario, and I was dressed in my most formal uniform, complete with upturned stiff shirt collar. We had to stand and mingle, holding a plate of food in one hand and a full glass in the other, before sitting round a dining table. 'His table-manners must be watched' was scrawled and underlined in red across my report for that exercise.

By far the most enjoyable of all occasions was the Summer Ball, and it was there I met Adrienne. Group invitations were sent out to the nearby teacher training college at Alnwick Castle and to the nurses' hostel near Newcastle, so just after the appointed time of 7pm, coaches full of female nurses and teachers arrived at the officers' mess. It's no coincidence that most of the pilots on my course married either a teacher or a nurse.

It was a perfect setting. I was in my almost new, best RAF uniform and Adrienne, aged just eighteen, was in her ball gown for the first time. The officers' mess, though still with a very formal air, (forever thus!) was bedecked in flowers. A lavish buffet was laid out along one wall, donated mostly by the taxpayer, which seemed to make it taste even nicer. A small band in the decorated anteroom played the smoochy songs of the day. The setting, the music, our ages, it was all so romantic that I could easily have fallen in love with myself, and I probably did. I certainly fell in love with Adrienne, though with my looks it might have taken her a little bit longer. We gelled from the first minute, and for both of us the summer of '63 was perfect.

Alnwick Castle, where Adrienne and the trainee teachers lived and studied for three years, was beautiful, and had seen drama, intrigue, and romance over seven hundred years, which I think we added to in our own small way. The film *Becket*, starring Richard Burton and Peter O'Toole, was filmed there at about that time. Many evenings we hastily kissed goodnight in the shadows of that imposing backdrop before Adrienne scurried off through the gatehouse to beat the return-time curfew.

The hut I lived in was somewhat less beautiful, but it didn't matter, because here I was, fulfilling my dream of becoming an RAF pilot. Life for me in the spring and summer of 1963 was perfect. The weather was idyllic after the coldest winter for years. My days were either flying in the shiny Jet Provost, or spending summer afternoons with Adrienne on the beautiful, deserted sandy beaches of Northumberland. Castles punctuated the headlands, and our instant favourite, of which I later got a painting, was the fourteenth century Dunstanburgh Castle, which was mostly in ruins but well worth the walk along the beach.

Acklington was remote and getting to Alnwick Castle was a problem. My fellow trainee-pilot Les Bennet (later to be my best man) also had a girlfriend training at the Castle, so we decided to buy a car together. We caught the bus into Newcastle and within thirty minutes had bought a shiny black Hillman Minx off the forecourt of a dodgy car dealership tucked away in the back streets. We asked few questions, because neither one of us knew anything about cars, and couldn't think of any to ask. But the car looked as though it would impress the girls.

We realised the dealership was dodgy only when the car ran out of oil and water in the centre of Newcastle, twenty minutes after we bought it. With help we got it going, but week by week the colour changed from shiny black to rusty brown, and one of the wings flapped as we went along; something a concerned policeman pointed out before filling in the charge-sheet. However, it did sort of work, and it did impress the girls.

The RAF station at Acklington was the perfect place to learn to fly. It seemed separate from the rest of the Royal Air Force and the cares of the world, and our yearly reunions in London are always well attended to this day.

I was sorry when my flying training came to an end. The culmination of it all, in true military style, was a parade at the station, when all new pilots were presented with their 'wings'. I could invite family and friends and I was happily surprised when some of my family (my eldest two brothers and my parents) made the trek up north for the ceremony. I was able to proudly introduce Adrienne to them for the first time, and I could tell that they liked her.

It was disappointing to hear a few years later that the impeccably kept airfield had become an opencast coal mine. Soon after that it was a prison. I loved my time at Acklington amid the hills and coastline of the county of Northumberland, so if I am ever called upon to do time I will choose to do it there, if only for the memories.

Now it was time for my first move, from Northumberland to Cambridgeshire, to complete my flying training on the twin-engine Vickers Varsity at RAF Oakington. I sold my share of the rusty Hillman and bought a more reliable Ford Anglia in which I could drive to see Adrienne, who still had two more years to finish her course at Alnwick Castle. I wasn't the only pilot there who wanted to see a trainee teacher, so it would always be a shared drive.

The Vickers Varsity was a lumbering old plane dating back from just after the war, and I think my love of flying half disappeared for the next few months. My attention was focused on Adrienne, and whenever possible I went to see her at Alnwick or when she was at home in Sheffield. Occasionally she came to see me and stayed in a little guest house outside Cambridge.

Despite its age, the Varsity was a reliable plane, and taught us how to fly with more than one engine (and more importantly, how to cope if one failed), how to navigate, which didn't concern us too much at Acklington, as well as getting us used to flying with a crew. That 'advanced' training lasted nine months, and then it was time to move again. I was off to RAF Thorney Island near Portsmouth, to fly the Blackburn Beverley, a gigantic and very noisy four-engine transport plane. It lumbered even more than the Varsity, but it flew a lot further, and within a week I'd left the UK for the first time in my life.

To see Gibraltar was an eye-opener for me, but things were really looking up; not long after I was doing 'circuits and bumps' around the airfield at El Adam in Libya. I'd joined the Air Force to see the world, and now I was doing it. On the ground too, things were taking off, with my second RAF Summer Ball. It was just as lavish as the first, and I invited several of Adrienne's family to join us… inch by inch I was becoming part of the Sheffield family.

It was just a four-month course at Thorney Island, before I was given my next move, to join 30 Squadron as a co-pilot and fly the big plane around the Persian Gulf from Bahrain. It sounded exotic enough to me, though a few months earlier it would have been even more so, because the squadron was moving from its old base in Nairobi Kenya. The only negative would be the separation from Adrienne, but she still had another year of her training to do, and I'd get back home as often as I could. On the 19 July 1965, Adrienne came down from Sheffield to see me off from RAF Lyneham in Wiltshire.

3

Though it was the early hours when I walked down the steps of the RAF Britannia plane at Muharraq airport Bahrain, it seemed unbelievably hot and humid, especially to somebody used to the weather of Maidstone in Kent.

I was welcomed by Flt Lieutenant John Wells from my new 30 Squadron, and it seemed he would be my mentor for the first couple of days. With the minimum of fuss, he showed me to my new home so that I could get a few hours' sleep. It was a hut, not unlike the one I'd had in Acklington, with a bedroom and a separate sitting area that included a writing desk. Thankfully it was air conditioned by a noisy electrical contraption on the wall. Muharraq was just a collection of aircraft hangars and wooden huts separate from the civil airfield that I could see in the distance.

Later that morning after a very decent breakfast at the officers' mess, I looked down the list that John Wells had given me. Nothing seemed too urgent, so the first thing I did was to return to my hut and meet my assigned Arab 'batman', who would look after my room for the next couple of years. Then I wandered around the RAF part of the airfield, until I found the 'Uniform Store', a fixture on every RAF station.

An obvious expert looked me up and down to judge my size, before giving me my KD (Khaki Drill), a full set of desert-type uniform. For the next two and a half years, air force blue was out and desert brown was in. I'd just become a Flying Officer so there was a slightly thicker stripe on my shoulders, but not yet thick enough to weigh me down, and I was still one of the most junior officers when I reported to my new squadron later that day. Before I could fly, I had to do 'dinghy drill', something done every few years in the RAF, but now especially important because of the vast expanse of the Arabian Sea we would fly over.

The next morning, I was sitting opposite John Wells again, this time in a dinghy as we drifted out to sea. The sun was still coming up, so it was all very cool and pleasant as John lay back and told me of his pre-RAF life, which was a lot more glamorous than mine. He and his sister Julie Andrews, of *My Fair Lady* fame, had been a theatrical double act, and he had lots of fascinating stories which he told well and to which I could have listened to all day, but they ended when an RAF speed boat crept up on us and we were told to inflate our life jackets and jump into the sea. We could see a helicopter approaching, and that would winch us aboard. Everything went seamlessly, largely because we knew there were sharks in the sea and couldn't wait to get out.

I decided that the Persian Gulf wasn't so bad, though the prospect of two and a half years seemed like a prison sentence. In the first few weeks a lot of our flying was back to the squadron's just vacated base at Eastleigh, Nairobi in Kenya, and I would rather have been there. Bahrain had its charm though, and I saw that it was changing rapidly, especially in the capital, Manama. There were donkey-drawn carts alongside big old American cars, high-rise buildings alongside minarets, and plans for a causeway across the water to Saudi Arabia.

Sadly, our airfield at Muharraq provided few attractions other than the flying. There was a beach near my hut, but it was littered with building rubbish and overshadowed by big electric pylons. We had guaranteed sun overhead, but the only place to lie in it was the Sheikh's beach near Manama. After Sheikh Khalifa ordered that single men had to be accompanied by a woman, the highlight of a non-flying day for me was a walk to the bar in the officers' mess and a game or two on the full-sized snooker table. I did that so often that I might have become a top snooker player and possibly an alcoholic.

RAF Station Muharraq came from the same template of every RAF station. The same three places called messes, where you could, depending on rank, eat, meet, and sometimes sleep.

I made my daily collection of Adrienne's eagerly anticipated airmail letters from the Muharraq officers' mess. We wrote to each other just about every day, and I still have literally hundreds of those flimsy lightweight letters in their red, white, and blue edged envelopes. Adrienne would keep mine in a small, battered leather case; I now handle the case and the letters, as fragile but very valuable.

The hot humid summers of the Persian Gulf meant flying was a welcome relief, though our 30 Squadron Beverleys didn't go high enough to get into the really cold air. But being low and slow brought good views of a unique landscape, something I enjoyed even more as a passenger on a VC10 flying back to England.

On the Beverley we usually headed down the Gulf from Bahrain, skirting the coast, unless dropping troops or supplies within the Arabian hinterland. Known as the 'empty quarter', it really was empty, the steep-sided sand dunes only occasionally dotted with a spec of green where water had somehow collected, and became a magnet for Bedouin tribes plodding slowly with their camels.

Our scheduled long flights were often cut short, because the Beverley's four big Bristol Centaurus engines couldn't cope. They used as much oil as fuel, so two extra eighty-four-gallon oil tanks were housed in the 'dog kennel', an area accessed through a circular hole at the very back of the cockpit between the wing spars.

It was the flight engineer's job to pump oil into the engines from the dog kennel every two hours, but if it was very hot the rest of the six crew would take turns. It was noisy in there, leading to long-term hearing damage that even the RAF later recognised. Engine problems were frequent, but sometimes were not a bad thing if they meant a diversion to an unintended airfield where we would get treats that we didn't get in Muharraq. Masirah Island, off the east coast of Oman, was a favourite diversion because of its open-air cinema.

The Persian Gulf had a dull loveliness to it, but the politics were often vibrant. The Arabs at that time were our friends, and the British regarded as fair arbiters for inter-sheikdom conflicts.

Our morning briefings were in the squadron headquarters, a hut, but on a grander scale with a badge on the front. The usual weather briefing might be followed by sketchy details of a 'problem' in the hinterland. The usual story of a fall-out between sheiks, possibly hid some input from the Foreign Office, but often led to a Beverley full of soldiers being dispatched an hour or so later to a carefully chosen piece of flat desert. They'd rush out the back of the plane as soon as we stopped, apparently knowing where they were going and what they were doing. There didn't seem time for much diplomacy but, as far as we knew, it was always mission accomplished. At night our desert landings were sometimes alongside a line of handheld petrol flares; scary for us, but much more so for the flare carriers on the ground, having to watch a big lumbering Beverley hurtle down towards them with lights blazing.

'Going on leave AGAIN Atkinson?' my squadron commander used to say before he signed my leave chit. It was something he said eleven times in my two and a half years. It irritated him, but just filling in that chit for leave gave me something to look forward to. In what I hoped was good-natured retaliation, whenever I left destined for the UK, he 'volunteered' me for a course that nobody else wanted to do. By the end of my two and a half years I was very well qualified in desert survival, sea survival, and interrogation. But it was all worth it, to get back to the UK, usually for only a week, to see Adrienne.

Flying back and forth to the UK would have been too expensive for a young Flying Officer in the RAF were it not for a scheme called 'indulging'. For a token amount I could hitch a lift on any RAF transport plane travelling with an empty seat. I imagine it was called 'indulging' just to make the users feel especially grateful. And I was, each and every time I took off in one of those empty seats from Bahrain on my way back to England.

It was often a bit last-minute; one time I ran still in my flying suit, suitcase in hand, to a just-about-to-depart VC 10 on the tarmac at Muharraq. However rushed, and it usually was, boy it was worth it once we were airborne and jetting westwards towards the UK. Unfortunately, the first stop was Akrotiri in Cyprus, where my seat was always wanted for a 'proper' passenger, so my indulgence stopped right there.

The first time I got a taxi to Nicosia and a very expensive BOAC ticket to London, all the while thinking it would be too costly to do often. Incredibly I found an insurance company willing to insure me against not being able to 'indulge' from Cyprus to the UK. It all seemed too good to be true, but for my next ten trips back and forth the policy paid my BOAC fare from Cyprus, all for a premium of £10 a year.

Those scrambled trips to go back home were a big effort, but the only way that Adrienne and I could spend some time together during those two and a half years. I would often baby sit in Bahrain, for a colleague two years older than me, with whom I trained, and who now lived very comfortably, with his wife in a provided house and with a sizeable marriage allowance added to his service pay. Their normal house in a normal street in a nice part of Manama was a welcome refuge from my service surroundings, and I couldn't help but compare their 'normality' in this very basic part of the world to mine. It wasn't just their house compared with my hut; it was their social life which contrasted sharply with my striving to get home every few months to see Adrienne.

After almost a year of being in Bahrain, on one of my short visits back to the UK, and as the days trickled away to the inevitable complications of the return journey, Adrienne and I wondered if there was an alternative. It was already clear that service life meant separation at short notice, and marriage under the age of twenty-five would make little difference, so it seemed that we had lost control of where we lived and even when we got married.

Perhaps we were young and impetuous, but we decided we would buck the system, ignore the magic age, and get married.

I have my letter to Adrienne from Muharraq, confirming that she definitely wasn't marrying for money; *I'm about to write to my parents telling them of our 6 August wedding date.*

My financial situation: I've got £225+ in the Midland and I'm about solvent here! So, things are looking up.

Her immediate reply was, *To my darling Alan. We think as one person and it's a marvellous feeling. There can't be anybody as smashing as you.*

Four months later she finished her time at Alnwick Castle and returned to her mother's house in Bents Drive, Sheffield, where she could make plans for our wedding.

On a gorgeous summer's day in August 1966 Adrienne and I married at Bents Green Methodist Church. My pilot friend from Acklington, Les Bennett, was my best man, and Adrienne was given away by her half-brother, George, head-master of the local Silverdale School. My parents were there and my two eldest brothers with their wives, but my other three siblings decided that Sheffield was either too far or they couldn't find somebody to look after their young children. Frances, my mother's great friend had made the effort to come from Edinburgh, just as she would to the same church fifteen years later for a very different occasion.

The church was full and, as I always hope for, the singing was loud. It was a perfect day for the convoy of cars to snake across the Yorkshire hills for the reception. Glasses were raised at the Scotsman's Pack, in Hathersage just across the border into Derbyshire, to wish us both a long and happy married life.

We'd agreed that Adrienne would organise the wedding and I would arrange the honeymoon. Perhaps it was sitting in that dinghy with John Wells telling me about his sister filming *The Sound of Music,* or perhaps because I liked the sound of the place, but I decided we should go to Salzburg. I had sought out the one travel agent in Manama and booked a hotel that overlooked Lake Traunsee in the Salzkammergut and took away the brochure that made it all look so wonderful.

I'd sold my Ford Anglia before I went to Bahrain, so on the day after our wedding I rented a car from London, and we drove down to Lydd Airfield in Kent. As promised by that travel agent in Manama, my ticket was accepted by Silver City Airways and we were flown, with our car, on a Bristol Freighter aircraft, smaller but similar to the Beverley, to Le Touquet in France.

We drove through France to Salzburg, stopping one night in Rheims. The ten days we spent in Austria were wonderful but over in a flash, and after agreeing not to talk about it on the way back to England, the dreaded day came; another indulgence flight back to Bahrain from the same airfield in Wiltshire, but this time I looked up the captain's name, went to his house and asked for his help in making sure I was definitely on.

That was something that could have backfired, but this return was emotional enough, without the added worry of not getting on the flight. It worked, and after another tearful goodbye on the tarmac I was heading westwards on the Bristol Britannia. Separating this time was made slightly easier as we had booked a BOAC ticket for Adrienne to visit me in Bahrain seven weeks later. That would fit in to her half-term holiday, because she was about to start teaching at an infant school in Sheffield.

Those weeks seemed a long time coming, but eventually in the early hours of an October morning, I watched Adrienne come down the steps of the BOAC VC10 in Muharraq. I had rented a small flat in Manama for the week, and a friend lent me his white Austin-Healey Sprite sports car. With the roof down on the little Sprite we explored the thirty-four-mile length of the island of Bahrain.

The capital Manama had a few high-rise buildings, but the rest of the island was mostly a sparsely populated desert. The only exception was the American town of Awali, which loomed out of the desert haze like a suburb of Virginia. Trees, pavements, shiny new buildings, manicured roads and even grass, all standing out like a sore thumb; Awali was a small but very rich town, built from the proceeds of a big oil refinery which processed oil from all over the Gulf. It was fascinating to see, but not to linger, because further down the coast was much more typical and memorable, where we found the people as unspoiled as the landscape. We were welcomed with big smiles and invitations to drink powerful coffee served from fire heated dallahs.

Our trip in the Sprite down the coast of Bahrain left lasting memories. We admired the people as much as the place, and the dhows drifting silently alongside long empty beaches was a centuries old image which I shared with Adrienne during our perfect week together.

I watched Adrienne depart in the VC10 for London, and I wished my remaining year in the Middle East would go quickly. In that time, I had another four short 'indulgence' trips to the UK, and we continued to keep the postal service busy between Bahrain and Sheffield.

I'm glad I had that week of discovery before I left Bahrain, because it completely altered my impression of everything. What I'd accepted as unremarkable and boring I now loved; in contrast to the bustling noisy country, I visited many times and many years later as an airline pilot. Though the RAF station had closed, on a far corner of an expanded Muharraq airport I located my old hut, now looking very forlorn, and a totally derelict officers' mess.

I spent almost two and a half years flying the Beverley (as my ears would testify) but the best came last, because right at the end of my time in Muharraq somebody decided that those giant slow-moving planes would be less visible if they were camouflaged. As with the lavish RAF Summer Balls, this was bad news for the taxpayer but good news for us, because the painting had to be done in Hong Kong. One by one our planes had to be flown there, and we were anxious to get going before there was a change of plan.

I set off on 29 January 1967, with a first stop in Bombay, and the second in Calcutta. That was two days, and things seemed to be going well, for a Beverley. The next leg was to Singapore, and our route took us almost overhead Bangkok. Just after getting airborne an instrument relating to one of the four engines started fluctuating and then stopped reading. All other indications were normal and our flight engineer's initial verdict was that there was nothing to worry about because the engine was running normally. Instruments, like everything on the Beverley, including us, vibrated as we went along because of those big Centaurus engines, and instruments sometimes succumbed. As we got closer to Bangkok, we talked about the attraction of diverting there to get the instrument fixed; even the air quartermaster, as he came up the cockpit ladder with sandwiches and coffee, reminded us what a great place Bangkok was, hinting probably in jest, that future sandwiches might not be as good if we overflew Bangkok.

We diverted into Don Mueang Airport, expecting to be there for a day or two, but that stretched into a week. The wrong replacement instrument was sent over and over again, to the angst of our flight engineer, but to the delight of the rest of the crew. It was my job, as co-pilot, to leave the five-star hotel every morning after a large breakfast to collect funds from the British Embassy. Our meals were paid for, and always accepted gratefully, with a wave of the hand, and a loud, 'The Queen will pay. '

We deserved our treat in Bangkok, because after two days in Singapore the next stop was Saigon, for fuel, at the height of the Vietnam War. On 12 February 1967 our Beverley landed in Saigon on a very foggy morning, and it was chaotic. Planes came out of the fog from left and right, and talk on air traffic control was non-stop, with chit-chat from the call-sign equivalents of 'Maverick', 'Goose' and 'Stinger', many years before the original *Top Gun*.

As I was to find out later as an airline pilot in the USA, it was difficult to get a word in edgeways and we were grateful to land, though that was traumatic. Our captain was somewhat deaf, but after we'd come to a stop not far down the runway, he obviously heard something which made him slam all four engines into reverse, and our big Beverley loomed out of the fog, in reverse, towards a plane that was about to land.

Reverse was cancelled and we headed onwards, eventually leaving the runway unscathed. We were all pleased to refuel and get away from Saigon, and it wasn't until we crossed the border of Vietnam that things calmed down. It was especially good to hear the soothing colonial voice of the Air Traffic Control at Kai Tak Airport, Hong Kong. The journey from Bahrain had taken us over two weeks, but it was two weeks of fun as well as excitement. Our flight back to Bahrain two days later was in something much quicker than a Beverley.

Just seven months later it was decided that our expensively

camouflaged planes should be flown back to the UK to be scrapped. Although I welcomed the decision to go home, the sudden demise of the Beverley was sad. As lumbering, oil-consuming and deaf-making as the plane was, it did an important job for the RAF and the Army, which its immediate replacements could never quite match.

I was going home four months earlier than planned. The squadron had farewell celebrations, and on the customary pewter tankard presented to me I had engraved the words *July 65-Sept 67, but it seemed longer*. Very truthfully it did, and despite the many plusses of living in a very different part of the world, it was good to be going home.

The journey back was lengthy, with the usual technical hiccups. In Cyprus I got news that Adrienne's mother had died suddenly, making me even more anxious to get back. Eventually we did, but only after a three-day enforced technical stop in Malta. I left my Beverley at its last resting place and caught something much more reliable, a train to Sheffield, where Adrienne was waiting for me.

I was a different person from the one that set off over two years earlier quite apart from the ingrained suntan and high-tone deafness. I'd become a married man and now Adrienne and a life together were the top of my priorities, above flying and everything else; and I wasn't sure whether the RAF and its drop of a hat postings would fit into that. However, there was much to look forward to, my two and a half year 'exile' was over and even the RAF's archaic magic age of twenty-five was not too far away. In October 1967 we looked forward to spending the rest of our lives together.

4

I was free from my uniform for a few weeks in Sheffield, while the RAF decided what to do with me. Paramount above everything was the death of Adrienne's mother and the planned funeral at Bents Green Methodist Church, in Sheffield where we had celebrated our wedding eleven months earlier. It was a big and sad gathering, but Adrienne's mixture of common sense and kindness shone through the gloom. For the first time I saw that she was the new natural hub of the family, and her mother would have been proud.

I awaited news from the RAF, hoping they had forgotten about me. They hadn't, and to make doubly sure, their telegram was quickly followed by a letter, all written in the same clear, no-nonsense way, with never a wasted word. I was to report in two weeks to RAF Topcliffe in North Yorkshire, and I could either find my own accommodation, or live in the officers' mess at Topcliffe. It took two seconds to decide that Adrienne and I would find a place to rent in North Yorkshire, very much aware that in just six months I would turn twenty-five and things would get easier, with subsidised accommodation provided.

We soon found a flat to rent, near Topcliffe, in the market square of Thirsk. It was the end part of a rambling old house, with a *Jane Eyre*-ish feel about it, the antique dark wooden furniture matching dark wood on the floors and the panelled walls. When I climbed down the stone steps to the cellar to replenish the big boiler with coal, I thought about my father's

Charles Dicken's books. But it was our first shared home, in a lovely small town, and we loved it.

We had few belongings, so very quickly we were settled in while I joined the Northern Communications Squadron at Topcliffe Airfield. Very soon after that, Adrienne was teaching infants at Carlton Miniott village primary school.

I was flying a twin-propeller plane called a Basset, which I had never heard of until I arrived at Topcliffe. With a navigator beside me, and five passengers behind, we flew politicians and service people around the UK and Europe, often with one or two nights away. Especially on dark winter nights, Adrienne didn't like being alone in our flat, but I often managed to exchange flying schedules with a colleague who flew most of my longer trips. That happy arrangement didn't last long, because after seven months I was moved again, this time to Bovingdon in Hertfordshire. We hadn't been in North Yorkshire long, but we both loved it, and the mark it made on me in those first few months would draw me back thirty years later.

My move to Bovingdon would be different because I was now twenty-five. I would be offered a subsidised house on the RAF station, (called a 'quarter'), as well as a marriage allowance. Ironically, I declined the quarter because we had decided to buy a house, an anchor that would steady the turmoil of constant RAF moves. I was 'signed up' for another twelve years but would keep my ears open for an opportunity to leave. As our new house was only half finished, we were invited to stay with our friends Peter and Yvonne who had also recently been moved down from Topcliffe to Bovingdon and had just moved into their own new house.

Little Spring, Chesham, we thought had a nice ring to it,

and when we moved to Number 8 in the summer of 1968, we couldn't have been happier. Everybody in the road was just like us; of similar age, newly married and buying their first home. And soon, it seemed, expecting their first child. We were the first, followed by our next-door neighbours, Alan and Margaret Brown. The four of us got on so well, we set up a tin-can intercom between the houses, which seemed to work, though we never knew why.

The two pregnancies were sort of shared, which helped both Adrienne and Margaret, and I chipped in where I could by learning all the breathing exercises and rehearsing them meticulously with Adrienne a couple of times a day. We did all we could to ensure that Nigel James was born without difficulties at Amersham Hospital on 13 October 1969; a date permanently imprinted on my mind. We quickly decided the names but thought carefully about who to have as godfather. In the end we chose Alistair M, a man who, for very different reasons, plays a significant part in this story.

Alistair was not only a cousin to Adrienne, but they shared the same birthday and he had lived most of his life just a few doors away in Bents Drive Sheffield. His mother, Iris, was married to the brother of Adrienne's mother, and Iris and Adrienne had a sort of mother-daughter relationship, Adrienne being the daughter that Iris never had. But she doted on her one son, Alistair, and when I came into the family he was already an intelligent and impressive character. Too intelligent, I used to think, at Iris's annual Christmas parties.

Every year without fail he won the big memory game of the night; *I packed my trunk and in it I put…* and I'm ashamed to admit that his repeated winning did irritate me. Those parties or that game could well have sown the seeds for our always at arms-length relationship; something severely tested in later life. His family and Adrienne's were closely intertwined, and we saw a lot of Alistair then, and later of his wife Sue. He was destined for great things, beyond being annoyingly good at Christmas party games, and Adrienne and I thought he would make an excellent godfather to Nigel.

Flying the Basset now from Bovingdon was more varied than from Topcliffe, and more interesting. The Basset was never a showstopper, but I was asked to fly it at the Finningley air show in 1968, where Adrienne's brother Howard and family came to watch me.

Bovingdon brought a string of nostalgic flights, the first to RAF Ouston in Northumberland, where seven years earlier I'd nervously flown my first solo. Then to Acklington, the beginning of my RAF flying days. But by a mile most evocative of all was my Basset flight to RAF West Malling Airfield in Kent, a lifetime since I'd been carried there on the crossbar of my brother's bike. Most rewarding, if in a small way, was a flight to Manston Airfield in Kent, near where my third brother Derek lived. We met up in the officers' mess and I reminded him of the night before I joined the RAF, when he bet me £5 that I would never go solo. Here I was, with my plane, so he grudgingly gave me the £5.

It all became slightly more serious when I started flying the Basset from RAF Northolt, to the west of London. We occasionally had junior government ministers sitting in the back, and I only mention Roy Hattersley because I always made a point of looking for his bright red socialist socks.

More memorable was the flight I made on 11 November

1969 from Northolt to Paris Le Bourget to mark the fiftieth anniversary of the first public overseas airmail service. That was also from London to Paris on 11 November 1919, so on that anniversary we carried Royal Mail first day covers to commemorate the event.

Alas, all good things come to an end, and after three very happy years living in Little Spring, the RAF wanted me to move once again. This time we had our home as an anchor, the place we could come back to, so we hastily arranged to rent it out, and the three of us moved into my first and only quarter, at RAF Colerne, in Wiltshire.

The semi-detached house in Cypress Walk, a road lined with hawthorn trees, felt good from the start, and all my doubts about living in an RAF house on an RAF station quickly disappeared. Everything seemed very easy and Adrienne soon immersed herself in RAF life, with its rules, traditions and obligations, quickly becoming friends with other young mothers living on the station.

The RAF had more pilots than it needed, and for me that meant no flying for the next two years, and a daily sixteen-mile drive from Colerne to the operations centre at RAF Lyneham. Despite that, life was good, and we were very happy, especially when Adrienne discovered she was pregnant again.

Living on an RAF station meant everything was done 'in house', so her medical checks were all at the nearby RAF hospital at Wroughton, and generally I would stay in the car with Nigel, who was then almost two, while Adrienne saw the doctor. On one visit, as she walked back towards me, I had a premonition of what she was about to say; she was expecting twins.

It was terrific news for us, and to our friends and relations when we rang to tell them. Except for my mother and father. My mother said, 'Oh dear,' and my father, in the background, 'Oh no, surely not.'

I was used to my family throwing cold water over things that I did, and in fact I always expected it, but I still had to take a couple of deep breaths.

Afterwards, I thought about their reticence, and decided it was just a harp back to their own early married life, when they struggled to cope with an ever-expanding family on a lorry driver's wage in a council house. They meant no harm, and after persuading them that we could manage and prosper from it all, they joined in the happy anticipation. Their reaction may have showed how ill-equipped they were to cope with my predicament a few years down the line.

On 18 April 1972 I was there when Anna-Jane and Lucy-Claire were born, a very emotional moment. It was almost two and a half years after Nigel, a gap we thought ideal, and now as a family we were complete. My mother had got over the shock of it all and showed how delighted she was by coming down to Colerne to stay for a week after the birth. That was particularly significant to me, because it was the most my parents had been separated in their long-married life, and it reflected how uniquely fond my mother was of Adrienne. There was little emotion shown in my house growing up, and the kiss Adrienne gave to my mother on meeting her that very first time was a bit of a watershed, and fixed Adrienne as special in my mother's affections.

Things were hectic for the first few months, especially when I had to work through the night, as I sometimes did. But I helped when I could, and Adrienne was always well organised and instinctively good at looking after children.

Alistair's mother Iris came down from Sheffield every few weeks and, as well as being a tremendous help to Adrienne, she developed a loving and quite unique bond with my children that would never change. Living on the RAF station was actually a help, because other young mothers were nearby, and as the girls got older, things got easier. We were grateful that all three were 'easy' children and having twin girls who would play together certainly helped.

Though hectic, life was just about perfect, and became even more so when I was asked to move again, because it meant a return to our house in Chesham. We had left as three and now returned as five, and life back in Little Spring continued as if we had never left. This was a happy stable family life, just as Adrienne and I wanted, and for us stability was the watchword. That unfortunately meant trying to leave the RAF. I had been given a three-month assignment as assistant project officer for a big recruiting exhibition in Birmingham called 'Meet the RAF 1973'; slightly ironic, now I was trying to leave. I was based at Stanmore in Middlesex and given an RAF-blue Morris 1800 staff car to drive, complete with red, white and blue roundels on the front and back.

The public relations and marketing side of the RAF was new to me, and I found it interesting. My naivety proved useful in that I could see things differently from those who had always lived it. The exhibition was dotted with expensive audio-visual dioramas, all with standard (boring) voiceovers. I thought that the actor Kenneth Moore and his association with the Douglas Bader biopic *Reach for the Sky* could provide the distinctive voice that would make all the difference. I got his agent's name and eventually spoke to the man himself. 'No charge old boy, just pick me up and drop me off.' That's what I did, and he breezed into the studio to do our voiceovers as many times as we wanted.

I wandered around the country with a photographer, recording little-known aspects of service life, including a stunning day aboard one of the RAF's Nicholson 55 yachts. I had no idea that the RAF had boats as well as planes.

I had to drive to the exhibition site in Birmingham two or three times a week. One summer's day I needed to drive up for what I knew would be a brief meeting. My route took me close to home, so I decided to collect Adrienne and the children and give them a day out in my staff car. Something I thought might be against the rules, but I was new to staff cars and wasn't sure. As a precaution against being seen by anybody who mattered, I took a cross-country route, avoiding the main roads, which made the journey even nicer.

Coincidentally, my station commander at Stanmore, in his bigger staff car with a flag on the front, set off at the same time from his house to the airfield. On such a nice day, he told his driver to take a cross-country route instead of the main roads. The result was that we passed each other on a tiny country lane. As I looked in my mirror, I could see my boss looking backwards towards me. Next morning, as expected, I was summoned to his office, and escaped with a warning that I was never to take passengers in an RAF car again.

My sights were now firmly set on leaving the RAF, with the goal of becoming an airline pilot. But I hadn't flown for over a year and thought I should get my flying up to date. My neighbour and RAF friend Peter Shaw was a very keen aviator, to the extent that on his days off and in the middle of the night, he flew newspapers to Europe from London. I joined him one night, meeting just after midnight in a hut away from the main buildings at Heathrow. It was bitterly cold and I noticed pyjama bottoms poking out of each of his trouser legs. He had more than one shirt on as well as a thick jumper, and that's when he told me that the plane's heater would not be working on the flight down to Zurich.

It was the middle of January, and once we scrambled on board I could see that some of the instruments in the little twin-engine plane were not working either, though apparently, they weren't important.

It got colder as our plane climbed higher, and I don't think I really cared if the instruments worked or not as long as we got to Zurich quickly. Get there we did, and helped to offload the newspapers in a temperature below zero. Once back to Heathrow and home, and thawed out in a hot bath, I vowed not to leave the RAF unless it was for a big airline. Ideally it would be BEA or BOAC, and certainly I wanted to fly planes where everything worked.

Then the chance came. I was working at both the recruiting centre in London and the exhibition in Birmingham. 'Numbers coming in and numbers going out' were very pertinent to recruiting, and I kept an eye on the ones going out. Senior officers confirmed a surplus of pilots, and that there might shortly be an opportunity to leave, albeit without a gratuity or a pension. Giving up a secure job with a young family and a mortgage was a risky thing to do, made worse if I sacrificed my pension. But I was contracted to eight more years of enforced moves, and stability and control were top of our wish list. At my age, and with a loving family behind me, I thought I could do anything, so I resigned from the RAF, and got confirmation that I could leave, after ten-years' service, at the end of the Birmingham exhibition in the April of 1973.

I knew that British European Airways were looking to recruit fifty pilots. I applied, and after a couple of interviews, got accepted to fly as a co-pilot on the Vickers Viscount. The condition was that I had to update my flying licences before joining. As a big contrast to the pre-ordained moves in the RAF, I had a choice of base; Birmingham, Glasgow or Jersey. Living in Jersey was a money-spinner because of the low tax, but instead we opted for Glasgow, mainly because our friends Peter and Yvonne Shaw were already there and enthusing about Helensburgh, a beautiful town on the banks of the Gare Loch.

The next few weeks were frantic. The exhibition was about to be opened by the Queen, but I needed to update my flying licences before I could join British Airways. That meant passing a flying test (my civilian flying Instrument Rating) and a very lengthy written Airline Transport Pilots Licence examination. It was a tight squeeze but I did it, helped by our neighbours in Little Spring who went away on holiday and let me sit in their quiet house to study. The biggest pressure was the cost of it all, having just given up my salary.

I flew my Instrument Rating test in a little plane from Stapleford Tawney Airfield in Essex, constantly reminding myself that one hours' flying equalled the cost of a refrigerator. Those words must have concentrated my thoughts, because though I hadn't flown for a couple of years, I passed the test first time.

The 15 November 1973 was a milestone for our family of five. I joined British European Airways and became an airline pilot, and from now on we were a stable family, choosing where and when we would move. More than that, we were a stable loving family looking to the future.

We sold our much-loved little house in Chesham, and moved to Firlands, in Upper Colquhoun Street, Helensburgh. It was perfect timing because Nigel was just four, and almost ready to start school.

First ever solo in the Jet provost at RAF Ouston, 7 August 1963

5

Helensburgh in Dunbartonshire is on the west coast of Scotland, on the northern shore of the Gare Loch, just at the point where it splits three ways. If you looked eastwards, it was along the River Clyde to Glasgow, westwards and you'd often see a submarine from the naval base at Faslane, and south westwards the water flowed round the tip of Ayrshire and out to sea.

Our new home looked down towards the town and the loch and was opposite Hill House, designed and built by the architect Charles Renee Mackintosh. Firlands was nowhere as grand as the house opposite, but we knew instantly that our friends Peter and Yvonne were spot on, we had moved to the right place.

I had a wonderful young family, and especially now with the extra chores involved in moving in, I was pleased to find that flying with BEA, at least for now, was not at all hectic. I flew so seldom that I suspected our new neighbours thought I was unemployed. When I did fly it was usually early in the morning before they were up and about, which was perfect for me because it meant a peaceful drive to work, alongside the loch towards Glasgow.

Nigel was about to start at Hermitage Primary School, only a short walk down small quiet crisscrossing roads, and lined in spring with pink and white cherry blossom. He was the apple of both his parent's eyes, as well as those of his twin sisters, so his first day at school loomed large for all of us. On the big day Adrienne and I were both there, looking at his class teacher and thinking what a big responsibility she had, to keep our precious son safe. Nigel took it all in his stride, and it was a lovely school that I still keep in touch with.

Joining Nigel's class was a little girl called Louise Risk, and on that first day we met her parents, Alison and Ralph. Louise was in Nigel's class throughout his time at the school and our families were together on most days during the next seven years. Helensburgh was a wonderful family orientated small town and had the lovely trait we had found living in Thirsk; you didn't have to make an appointment to visit somebody, you just popped around, and as often as not, a drink was soon in your hand.

Two years passed very quickly and it was time for the girls to start school. We were all excited, especially the twins. They gave each other confidence, but they still looked to their big brother, who would never be far away. As with Nigel, Adrienne and I were both there on that first day, looking the teacher up and down hoping she could be entrusted with looking after our precious duo. We soon found she could be and the school was fantastic. My twins loved and looked to each other, Lucy's humour and confidence matched by Anna's poise and reticence.

Perhaps the only downside we could find, (or *I* could find, because the others didn't notice), was that Helensburgh had more than its fair share of rain. We made the most of the fresh sunny days and started new family traditions. The day the clocks went back in October was always, regardless of weather, the day for a long walk in Glen Fruin, a long valley just behind where we lived. Once the place where Clan MacGregor battled

Clan Colquhoun, it was our favourite place for family walks, and always on that Sunday in October. Traditionally, Nigel would ask the first sheep we saw, 'Is this the way to Maidstone?', exactly as my father had done on an early morning walk with him a couple of years before. We always followed the stream that eventually fed Loch Lomond, now moving slowly but in a few weeks, after the snows, would be a fast-flowing river.

That extra hour meant we were up '*bright and early*'. This was one of Adrienne's favourite expressions. People from the north of England tend to say it with particular expressiveness and enthusiasm, a sort of call to arms. Adrienne said it at that moment to encourage the family, now, this instant, to go for it and get cracking so that we had time after the walk for the short drive to Loch Lomond. The old village of Luss, on the western shore, was definitely Adrienne's favourite place. Usually, class-mates of our children tagged along, to skim stones across the surface of the water, or just to sit on the pebbles watching the loch from the water's edge.

For us, Loch Lomond had a magical feel, probably fueled by the islands and the ruined castles and the legacy of the warring clans. We thought it was beautiful, especially when those islands that held so much history stood out with bluebells or rhododendrons. 'Our place' on the edge of the water was 'tranquility base' for Adrienne and me, free of disturbance or sound to compete with our thoughts; invariably our shared pride of our children in front of us. Their happy laughter and the echoey sound of those stones skimming the water made Luss, as with Glen Fruin, 'our' family place. That's why Adrienne had decided to take our rented video camera there by herself and point it across the silent wintry loch. She can be

47

heard saying, 'This is what it's all about', and it was for both of us. The difference was, she was always calm and appreciated things as they were, whereas usually I didn't make time for that and instead dreamed of what might be.

I'm glad that we explored Loch Lomond to the full, even hitching a ride on the 'post boat' that delivered mail to the largest island, Inchmurrin. I treasure a photo of my family and Nigel's friend Mark, sitting on the top of a snowy Ben Lomond and looking over the loch. That photo sums up everything that our piece of Scotland meant to us as a family.

'*This is what it's all about.*'

Like clockwork, the rain turned to snow between Christmas and New Year, so with sledges in the back of our Saab it was off to the 'Rest and be Thankful' hill at Lochgoilhead. On that hill, on our last visit in early January 1981, I had a moment that lies indelibly in my mind.

We had sledged all afternoon, and as it got dark and cold, we retreated to our old Saab, to find the engine wouldn't start.

I remembered a farmhouse about half a mile down the lane, and with Nigel, set off to seek help. I was worried, but tried to appear calm, and looked across at my son as we trudged down the hill, which gave me the moment which stays in my memory. He looked tall and fit and strode confidently beside me, unfazed by the cold and dim light. He was just eleven, and I was thirty-seven, but for the very first time I felt a changing of the guard; perhaps I *was* getting old and vulnerable, but the young boy on my right was the future. From the farmhouse we phoned the AA, and although we were miles from anywhere, somehow, they had our old Saab working almost by the time Nigel and I got back to it.

New Year usually brought snow to Helensburgh, while July often brought rain. As the spectators at Wimbledon complained about the heat, I looked outside and complained about the downpour. We needed to escape for just two weeks in July, and soon we could, because our close friends Alex and Chris had a caravan at Fréjus, in the South of France. We rented it for the same two weeks every year, enabling holidays that were as simple as they were great, with the journey a looked-forward-to part of it all. For six consecutive years we flew from Glasgow to Nice, where we rented a Citroën 2CV (a different colour every year) from the same Citer rental desk. With the hood on the car rolled right back, we drove along the coast to our caravan, stopping just occasionally to look at the sea or buy ice creams.

Traditionally, at some point, Lucy and I sang our version of the Bonnie Tyler song; 'Lost in France' to which we always added 'with my little girlie Lucy'. To placate Anna in case she felt left out, we then sang to the *Archers* signature tune, 'Anna-Jane's a lovely girl, and so's her sister Lucy'. All with the hood right back so possibly others joined in the chorus. They were the happiest of all times.

Le Domaine du Pin de la Lègue caravan site was well situated for any young family, not far from Fréjus but more importantly just a short walk to the sea. Our neighbours in the next caravan, Sally and Richard from New Malden, were yet to have children, but instantly gelled with ours. We spent long happy days on the beach together, with Richard patiently repeating his magic tricks and playing games with the children. We became friends for life.

One day I'd seen and translated a poster in the old Roman town. It was advertising what I interpreted to be an open-air opera in the Arènes de Fréjus, a large Roman amphitheatre.

I wanted to see the arena more than the performance, but we decided to go. With Richard and Sally looking after the children, we set off in the 2CV, suitably dressed for a night at the opera. As others filed in, they didn't look like opera goers, but this was France. Once the arena was full there was a loud trumpet fanfare, heralding not singers but a bull. We were at a bullfight, not an opera. We swiftly left. The reading of French as well as the speaking of it, was now to be left to Adrienne, who was good at everything I wasn't and a lot more bedsides. What would I have done without her?

With all the children at school I was free to do more things on my many days at home. I joined the local sailing club and bought a secondhand GP14 dinghy. I didn't venture far on the loch, because I really didn't know what I was doing, but occasionally on a calm day and with lifejackets on, I took Nigel out for a short sail. We went cautiously, and not very far, towards the upturned hull of a Greek sugar boat that lay on a sandbank after capsizing in a storm two years before. It seemed to mark the centre of the loch and a good place to aim for, though we never reached it. Instead, once away from the shore, I would lower the sails and we'd drift, me puffing a small Hamlet cigar, and both of us taking in the splendour of our surroundings.

Adrienne thought we should have a dog, and we bought Sophie, a tri-coloured Cavalier King Charles Spaniel. The children instantly loved her, but I was uncertain, for the first week or two, to say the least. After being soaked once again taking Sophie for an early morning walk, I put an advertisement in the *Helensburgh Advertiser, Dog for sale to good home*. More of a protest than anything else, I underestimated the speed with which it would appear in the paper.

I was in the loft setting up Scalextric for Nigel and probably thinking how I would tell Adrienne, when I heard the telephone ring. Adrienne, downstairs with a friend, said, 'Wrong number.' When it rang again and again, I knew my game was up.

Quite reasonably, I thought later, she took away the loft ladder and left me imprisoned for a few hours. I did have a Scalextric to play with, but I couldn't stay up there forever, and after apologising a hundred times and agreeing to keep Sophie, she set me free. Needless to say, it wasn't long before I came to love Sophie like everybody else, and she really was the sixth member of our family.

As the children got older, we became busier. Sunday afternoons for Adrienne and I meant watching the girls learn to horse ride on the hill overlooking the loch. We were often frozen by the wind off the water as they trotted up and down, then round and round. Then up and down again, and again. They loved it, though Lucy got exasperated by my weekly question as she got on her horse; 'Have you filled up with petrol?' Her weekly reply was, 'Don't be so silly, Daddy', while Adrienne just rolled her eyes.

We were deep into Helensburgh life. Nigel enjoyed his Cubs, and the girls their Brownies, with Adrienne methodically sewing on the badges and me usually taking the children and bringing them back. Adrienne frequently went to the Glasgow Auction Rooms with Alison Risk, and the 'bargains' Adrienne bought became bigger and bigger until we acquired a baby grand piano. It needed serious re-polishing but led to the children having weekly piano lessons.

They persuaded me to give it a try, so an extra half hour

with their teacher Mrs. Kelso was tagged on to the children's lessons. I knew I wasn't a natural, but even so I was deflated when I heard Mrs. Kelso ask Lucy-Claire, my seven-year-old daughter, to explain something to me. She did, in her 'Mrs. Kelso' broad Glaswegian accent, which Lucy could speak at the drop of a hat. I had already decided that it was all beyond me and I was grateful when a dropped paving slab on my finger brought an end to my piano playing career.

Adrienne loved teaching infants but, after growing up along-side her brother Peter, who had Down's syndrome, she felt destined to teach special needs children. He was a big part of her life and she had a love and an understanding of him that nobody else had. When her mother died Adrienne happily took over the responsibility for Peter, which could have been a problem when we moved from Sheffield a year after getting married. She searched long and hard for exactly the right home, and her lifelong involvement with the Sheffield Society for the Mentally Handicapped helped her to do that.

She found Oakbrook View, a small care home not far from where she lived. With Peter we went to have a look, and after meeting the wardens, Mr. and Mrs. Smith, who lived on site, we knew it was exactly the right place. They kept a parental eye on everything and everybody, and Peter was immediately happy there. Three times a week, he and his friend Keith caught the bus to a centre called The Towers, where they made cane-work stools and small tables, and his ever-happy demeanour, even in the bus queue, was seen and remembered by many. Wherever Adrienne and I lived Peter remained a strong part of our lives, and we took him on regular holidays with us.

Only now, with the children at school and me at home so

much, was it possible for Adrienne to get the extra qualifica-
tion she needed, which required taking a one-year course at
Jordanhill College in Glasgow. Luckily the course was only in
term time, but it wouldn't have been possible without having
our friends Alison and Ralph Risk on essential standby to look
after the children for an hour or two when needed. Their children were of similar age and at the same school, so both sets of
children were in each other's house much of the week anyway.

To look after three children at home and commute to
Glasgow for the course, was hard work for Adrienne but a
year later she had finished and became a peripatetic teacher
of the most severely handicapped special needs children. Such
teachers were scarce, and she was soon at work for four days a
week, though she always left home after the children left for
school and, if I wasn't there, returned to collect them from
school. On her working days, she drove to a special school near
Glasgow or to the homes of children who were too severely
disabled to attend even that school. Many of those were in very
poor and reportedly dangerous parts of the city, and initially
I went with her. But we soon knew there was absolutely no
need to worry; those parents had hearts of gold and were so
pleased to see Adrienne. Some of the children she visited were
in an almost vegetative state, and at the beginning, I naively
questioned what she could do, but Adrienne had found her
niche, and delighted in the slightest improvement which she
could see, and the parents could see, even if I couldn't.

I was a sort of house husband during that time, at home
with Sophie, doing jobs around the house and dropping off
and collecting the children from school. I thought it complete
bliss. I cooked lunch for them, often from a menu prescribed by

Adrienne, and it was usually Lucy who would tell her mother if it wasn't quite up to scratch, and Sophie our dog who enjoyed it most.

On his first day at school Nigel made friends with a class-mate, Mark Pattinson, and from then onwards they were inseparable, at each other's house, at cubs, at the swimming club or at Saturday morning rugby training. Mark became part of the family. They both had bikes and Mark now holds a 'Race Across America' cycle record. Those very close bonds bring home to me the distress that subsequent events caused to the Pattinson's lives as well as mine.

I once went with Nigel and Mark on a weekend father and son Cub camp in Dumfermline about sixty miles east of Helensburgh; Mark's father worked for the Navy and at the last minute was unable to come. We arrived on the Saturday morning and pitched our tent very quickly. The two days were full of activity for the Cubs who came from all over Scotland, with just the odd game in which I could take part. Adrienne and the girls joined us at the end of the second day, providing another snapshot moment in my life. All three of them had made great efforts to look wonderful for us, and how wonder-ful they looked. The girls wore their new tartan outfits and even Sophie wagged her tail appreciatively. It was one of those moments when it was clear that women (and six-year-old girls) could bring to the party an elegance and a civilised style that us men and boys could never quite manage, however much we tried. That weekend was memorable and, as on so many of those occasions it was good to have Mark with us, as one of the family. *(Only recently did I find a letter from Mark sent to me asking if he could be my 'honourable' godson! I wish I had read that letter earlier. It would have been a great fillip for me, and of course I would have agreed.)*

The seventies ticked by and life was good for all of us. Adrienne was fulfilled in her job, and we were both happy in our family. We even sold the old 'Sammy' Saab and bought Iris's Audi, which she had been just about to trade in. Secretly I bought Adrienne a damask red MGB GT for her birthday, trusting the children to keep mum, though I knew that if anyone would tell her it would be Lucy.

On the big day I had the new car hidden in the garage and when the big moment came it seemed to be a total surprise; though a few moments afterwards I think I noticed a knowing look between Lucy and her mother. I enjoyed that she and Adrienne were special soulmates, as I was with her sister Anna.

The children were all doing well. We glowed with pride when we saw the teachers at Nigel's school, or read his yearly reports, which always said something like, 'Worked at a very high standard throughout the year'. One says, 'He is a very balanced child'. I can only wonder what might have been and I take a sort of inherited pride when I learned that his close friend Mark had become so successful on Wall Street.

Adrienne and I and his proud sisters watched Nigel do so many things, and he never let us down. We watched him in the school sports; play rugby and swim; and once the girls and I, (Adrienne had an important exam), in trepidation watched him at a special church service in Dumbarton in 1977.

It was to mark the Queen's Silver Jubilee, and just one boy and one girl from each age group in a very large area had been chosen to read a lesson. Nigel was chosen, and he practiced on our stairs. On the big day the Church was huge and daunting, full of children, teachers, and parents. I felt nervous when Nigel strode up as the first to read. As always, he looked the part, smartly dressed, standing tall and straight with his fair hair shining. He read beautifully. Nigel was wonderful and he is still my hero in life.

The girls were younger, and wonderful in an equal but different way. They didn't have the same competitive edge but were both doing well and had their whole class at their birthday parties in April. I knew all of them from Class P3, from sweet and gentle Julie-Ann *(later to become CEO of a large building society)* to the more boisterous Gordon McGregor who looked a likely candidate for tossing the caber. Their three Chinese classmates, Chick Lee, Pu Na Lee, and Chu Wang, names I still remember, were neat and perfect in everything that they did and didn't seem to notice that my pronunciation of their names (as instructed by Lucy) wasn't anywhere near as perfect.

We spent the Christmas of 1979 with my parents in Maidstone. For the first time, I saw an unusually mellow side to my father, and they both showed the real love they had for Adrienne and our children. The energy and thought they devoted to ensure the children had such a lovely Christmas was wonderful at the time and comforting in the years ahead.

In February 1980 we decided to escape from the cold, and I wanted to go to the USA for the first time. I hadn't used my staff-discounted tickets, and the children's half-term was coming up, so we thought we'd try to go to Disneyland in Los Angeles. The tickets were 'standby', so nothing was absolutely certain.

We left '*bright and early*', from Helensburgh, and caught the shuttle flight from Glasgow to Heathrow. Things worked out beautifully. Our standby tickets became first class, and I could scarcely believe how different this standby travel was to my indulgence flights in the RAF. It seemed in no time at all we were jetting across to San Francisco for our week in the sun and my first look at America.

I hired a big American car at San Francisco Airport from the first rental desk I saw, *Dollar Rent A Car*. (Later a significant name in this story). We booked ourselves in for two nights at a hotel in San Francisco and spent two days enthralling the children (and ourselves) with the city. Then in our big American car, we drove up the Pacific Coast Highway to Los Angeles and Disneyland. The children loved every minute, and we all had a wonderful holiday on our first venture far afield. Perhaps it was the success of it all that inspired us to do something similar exactly one year later.

Adrienne. Always the perfect wife and mother

Part two

Mix pictures of the mind, recall
That table and the talk of youth

6

Adrienne and the children had found their niche in Scotland and wanted to stay where they were. I wanted to change things and to move down south, for reasons that seemed very reasonable at the time but seem less so now.

British Airways had offered me the opportunity to fly jets, as opposed to the turboprop Vickers Viscount. Flying the Viscount around Scotland was very satisfying, but I had done it for seven years and it felt like it was time for a change. Not only that, but I'd been offered the chance to fly the shiny new Boeing 737. I would be based at Gatwick, to the south of London, meaning a family move, which would fit in nicely because Nigel would soon be eleven and due for a change of school. If we were going to move, now was the time.

For more profound reasons Adrienne was arguing to stay. She was supported by all the many friends that she had made, and I suspect especially by our friend Yvonne, who was having the same argument with her husband Peter. With hindsight I can see that Adrienne was right; we had something going for us in Helensburgh that money cannot buy, and sunnier weather couldn't bring. We had extreme happiness in a lovely part of the world; Nigel could have moved to the school that all his friends would have gone to, and I could even have flown the shiny jet whilst continuing to live in Scotland. It would just have meant commuting up and down by air from Gatwick to Glasgow (using free tickets provided) and finding somewhere to stay near Gatwick between flights when there wasn't time to get home. Others were doing it but... I'd left the RAF to put family life first, and now with three lovely children as well as a lovely wife, why would I want to work four hundred miles away from where they all lived?

I had to decide. As luck, or fate would have it, I was rostered for a flight in the Viscount down to Gatwick - an unusual route for us. As we flew south, we left cloud behind, and as we circled to land at Gatwick I looked down at neat green fields and country lanes bathed in early summer sunshine. At that moment it seemed so obvious; this was an opportunity we had to take, but the children as well as Adrienne needed persuading. We called a family conference and gathered round the white circular kitchen table that I still have today.

Adrienne started by saying, 'Daddy's got some exciting news'. We usually had our meetings to decide where to go for our walks; along the seafront or to our favourite picnic spot in Glen Fruin. Or whether to go to Sheffield or to Maidstone at half-term. But this was different, and Adrienne's opening brought silence - the children were hanging on to every word.

'How would you like to move to where it is very sunny and near Grandad?' I asked. To spice it up a bit I added, 'Not far from the Queen at Buckingham Palace', which got the expected condescending look from Lucy, but a thoughtful look from Anna. That lightened things, and before long Lucy, was doing most of the talking and lapsing into her Mrs. Thatcher or a broad Glaswegian accent to make us all laugh. We talked about all the positives, and agreed that we really should move, but on condition that we would stay in touch with our (and their) friends. The decision was made, we were going south.

After telling British Airways that I wanted to change to the Boeing 737, they gave me the welcome news that most of the conversion course on to the new plane would be in Canada, and at the end of April1980 I flew to Vancouver to begin the five-week course. It was my first time there and I thought it wonderful, something echoed by an old couple from Yorkshire who had just retired to the city. 'Best thing we ever did', they said. I thought if it's better than Yorkshire it must be good.

My first impressions were that Vancouver was Helensburgh on a grand scale, with the mountains higher and more heavily snow-capped and the waters definitely bluer. It was a lucky coincidence that I'd sat next to my assigned course-training captain on the flight from London because I'd known Captain Brian Long for years. He oozed calm, even before going to the bar, and I knew I'd have to make a pretty big mistake to fail the course, so I was set fair.

We were given tickets to fly home for two weekends during the course, and I arrived back laden with gadgets for the children: two tents and a sledge, but best of all, rockets which when put together, launched hundreds of feet into the air. I'm not sure how legal they were, but we had several Cape Canaveral-type launches, counting down from ten to one, for the children and their friends.

The course was entirely in the classroom and the flight simulators which were owned by the Pacific Western Airline. Simulator time had to fit in with the demands of their own pilots, so often took place in the middle of the night. But the course was good fun, and I returned to London ready to fly the Boeing 737.

I reported to British Airtours, the charter side of British

Airways at Gatwick Airport to the south of London. The man in charge of the company's flying was Captain Bill Brennen, someone who would figure large in my life just a few months later. For the first time I flew the *actual* Boeing 737 as opposed to the simulator, without passengers until all my licence requirements were ticked off. On 8 June 1980 I began my commercial jet flying with a return flight to Malaga.

Because the summer flying schedules were hectic, I couldn't get back to Scotland as often as I wanted. Being separated from my family now was just as difficult as my enforced separation from Adrienne at the beginning of our married life, so I used most of my time off to search for a house in the south of England. I went into great detail, driving and walking many miles and even delving into town expansion plans because the population there was growing rapidly. I sought a house that was big enough for the five of us, near to good schools and not too far from the sea; in a part of the world that was small enough to be friendly but big enough to be buzzing. Like the house we were leaving in Helensburgh but with a bit more sun.

It was not long before I found just what I was looking for, on the top of a hill outside Steyning on the South Downs in Sussex.

Called Downsway, it was perched so high on the Downs that it overlooked the village, and at night (I was so obsessed with the house, I drove down there to check), I could see the village lights twinkling below. I got so carried away that I bought a book on how to build a wind turbine, anticipating that Nigel and I would build one, to use the wind off the hill.

I was in love with that house, more than any other before or since, and I couldn't wait to get home and enthuse the family.

Fortunately, they all seemed impressed, so the next step was for us all to fly down south to see it.

We flew on the shuttle from Glasgow Airport and hired a car from Gatwick. Our three days down south on a late summer weekend was an adventure in itself for the children, and we meandered in no particular hurry towards Steyning, briefly looking at Briarwood, a similar house for sale in West Chiltington. It was easy to decide against that one, and we continued our drive to the Bramley Grange Hotel near Haslemere in Surrey, where I'd booked a large family room.

My parents drove the short distance from Maidstone, and on a lovely day we all walked down to the River Wey. I rented two canoes, one for Nigel who could manage by himself and one for me, to take the girls in turn. Tactfully I didn't mention the temperature but hoped they noticed the slightly different climate down south. We were all together, the sun was shining, and we were full of expectation at seeing a house on the morrow that I'd waxed lyrical about. Sadly, it was the last time my parents saw Adrienne and their grandchildren.

I had all my fingers crossed as I approached Steyning the next day. Bostal Road was a narrow and twisty road that led across the Downs to the south coast, and near the top of the hill, past a sharp bend, we saw Downsway. The house and the swimming pool glistened in the morning sunshine, and I thanked heaven for the sun and thought anybody would love what they saw now. It was indeed love at first sight for all, and we were soon being shown around the house by the owner. The girls were deciding which beds they would sleep in, while Nigel and I looked at the pool. The final decision was unanimous; this was a house worth leaving wonderful Helensburgh for.

Adrienne and I talked about it on the way home, and she was as excited as I was. Our offer on Downsway was accepted and with more than a tinge of sadness, we saw the For Sale notice go up at Firlands. Hopefully we would move in before Christmas.

The whole project thrilled me and I could think of nothing else. I dreamt of our Saab, full to the gunwales crossing the border between Scotland and England. I couldn't wait, not because I didn't love Helensburgh, but because a change was inevitable, and we had stumbled upon the perfect place to live. I was the Grand old Duke of York; I'd finally got to the top of the hill.

We soon heard that the Steyning sellers couldn't wait either, because they were getting divorced, and they put pressure on us to exchange contracts. When September became December with no sign of our house being sold, our sellers began to lose patience. We were given a final deadline date for the contract of 1 February 1981, and we could only wait and hope.

Then it happened, and I'll always remember the moment. On a cold afternoon at the end of January, I'd just walked home from school with the children and Adrienne was on her way home from Glasgow. The telephone rang and I heard the words I'd been waiting for; 'There is a good offer on your house.'

Under the Scottish real estate system an offer is more or less set in stone. Our house was sold, just days before the deadline, and we could move to our dream house. I was over the moon and wanting to celebrate. As I always do when I'm very up or very down, I played my favourite music. Records went on the turntable and I danced around the sitting room cheek to cheek with Anna and Lucy in turn. 'By the time I get to

Phoenix' became, 'By the time I get to Steyning', and we were all singing when Adrienne walked in, to join me on the dance floor with Anna-Jane. We carried on for a long time, the girls wanting to play the Olivia Newton-John's songs from *Grease*, and Nigel wanting the Glaswegian Jimmy Shand and his Band. The girls put their kilts on for that; Anna-Jane's typically, was a beautifully coordinated grey-blue and Lucy-Claire's, typically, a very vibrant red. Fortune had smiled on us after making us wait. Due to the film 10 a massive hit at the time, Harvey Wallbangers were the drink of the moment, and only after quite a few of those did Adrienne and I go to bed, very happy, very settled and very optimistic about what was ahead of us.

Before moving there were many things to do. A large house, three young children and an untidy father meant lots of packing and sorting. But even before all that, we thought we should celebrate. School half-term was coming up, our short trip to San Francisco the year before had been a great success, so we would go once more to somewhere warm, using my BA staff standby tickets.

We were all on a high, so why not the Caribbean? Even the word had a nice ring to it, especially when I looked outside at the snow. We walked on air for the next few days, waiting for half-term to begin. The night before, we all said a fond farewell to our little dog Sophie, before I took her to Yvonne and Peter to be looked after for the week.

Next morning, we were all up '*bright and early*' for the drive to Glasgow Airport to catch the first shuttle flight to Heathrow. We had sold our Saab, and were now in the bright red Audi we had bought from Iris. The staff car park looked cold and almost deserted as we parked and lugged our cases over to the terminal. It was bad news: fog at Heathrow meant our flight was delayed, so we sat with our cases for a couple of hours, waiting for the fog to lift.

It was late morning when we eventually arrived at Heathrow, too late for our connection to Barbados. Trailing our luggage, we all walked round to the British Airways Staff Travel Office to see if we could salvage our holiday by going somewhere else.

What happened next, I have played over many times in my mind. I can picture the bespectacled slightly officious British Airways lady behind the counter, very aware that she knew all there was to know about staff travel, and that we knew absolutely nothing. We hung on to her every word, the children especially, because they definitely wanted to go somewhere exciting. Then came the fateful words, 'Why not go to Miami? The flight goes in two hours and there are lots of spare seats for your standby tickets.'

Wonderful, we all thought.

Though it turned out somewhat differently.

*

It was really by default that we went to Miami; the hand of fate that delayed our journey from Glasgow. Our decision to move, the last-minute sale of our house, the decision to celebrate; those events which we thought had fortuitously contrived together had in fact, placed all five of us on a flight to Miami Florida from which only I would return.

As we flew westwards, a certain Mr. Anderson was probably having his usual day, fishing at the Everglades, possibly drinking his cans of beer, before driving back home in his old, legally underinsured car.

7

Our eight-hour flight westwards on the giant Boeing 747 seemed an exciting harbinger for what was ahead, and we departed the plane as five tired but happy, enthusiastic travellers. The children were wide-eyed with what they were seeing, and all the while anticipating what was ahead.

We hadn't pre-booked a car, so as we waited in the busy terminal at Miami Airport, I had time to think back to last year's holiday and car rental. There, we'd quickly completed the rental desk paperwork, but I'd been surprised outside the terminal by the bigger than expected rental car. The all-American Chrysler had a front and back bigger than the whole of my little Audi at home and a strange gearstick protruding from the dashboard; I remember breathing a sigh of relief when we emerged unscathed from the four-lane melee outside San Francisco Airport. Now, waiting in the queue, I thought about what might happen if I collided with a rich, legally savvy American. This was a hectic country, and I needed good insurance.

At last, at the head of the queue with the rental form completed, I asked pointedly, 'Am I fully covered?' 'Yes, buddy you are,' was the agent's reply. I'd ticked every box except the $50,000 Personal Accident option, my fleeting thought being that I had enough life insurance on my own life.

Comforted by those words we ventured into the 'big country'. I drove our bright red Mercury two-door sedan and my four buoyant passengers, northwards from Miami towards our destination of Sarasota on the north-west Florida coast. We stopped for an hour at an almost deserted tidal island with talcum powder soft white sand and beautiful clear blue water. A desert island, the sort of place we read stories about to the children.

Despite all being tired after a long day, spirits were high when we checked in to the Holiday Inn Hotel, on the beach at Sarasota. Our family room had two big beds and a foldaway bed for Nigel. We were all safely together for what promised to be a week of fun and happiness, just wonderful for our short celebration.

The temperature was perfect, and the water was inviting to all of us, so we lounged, played, and swam for most of those five days. The children were enthralled by the American way of life, the larger-than-life enthusiasm and sheer over the top brightness echoing what they had seen back home on television. And the accents, that Lucy could soon mimic and mix with her Margaret Thatcher and broad Glaswegian to make us all laugh. It was the beginning of computer games, and Nigel and I finished our days on the beach with Space Invader competitions on the machine in the hotel lobby. The big family room was ideal, and we all slept soundly.

After a few tensions in the previous few months, mainly about the upheavals ahead of us, Adrienne and I felt as one again. We were at last looking forward together, so proud of each other and our lovely family and where we were in life. We couldn't wish for more than what we had, and for what we had to look forward to.

School half-term holidays were short, so it was soon time to drive back to Miami Airport for the late evening flight to

London. We checked out the hotel at midday but spent the afternoon on the beach and by the hotel pool, soaking up the sun before facing the cold weather of the UK. The large pool had a diving board, which Nigel was soon diving from, but the girls and I were a bit more circumspect. We eventually jumped, with absolutely no marks for style. After a while Lucy was happy enough to go by herself, but Anna, always slightly less confident, wanted to hold my hand. Secretly the board seemed quite high to me, and I was pleased to be holding *her* hand. Time and again we jumped off the board with lots of laughter, enjoying every second while Adrienne reclined and watched, and made the most of the sun.

But soon it really was time to go. Nigel and I quickly got changed but Adrienne said she would change the girls into their winter clothes in the car. It was late afternoon when we set off in our hire car, with Nigel in the front with me while Adrienne changed the girls in the back.

The sun was beginning to fade, and we decided to stop for food before it really did get dark. The children loved the fast-food places that seemed, and still seem, so much better in the USA than here. Denny's was their favourite, so when we came to the bright lights of Fort Myers, that was where we went.

I'm sure the meal wasn't memorable but engraved in my mind is crossing the road back to the car, clutching Anna's hand. As always, she instinctively slipped her hand into mine and at the same time looked at me intensely with her lovely blue eyes, confirming that we were soulmates. We were, always; at that moment I knew she was as happy as she could be.

Adrienne suddenly remembered that she had postcards to send and scurried off to a blue postbox on the next corner. The light of another flawless day had gone, and it really was time to start our two-hour drive back to Miami Airport, where we'd arrived just five short days ago.

After carefully settling the children into the back seat Adrienne strapped herself in next to me, pointing out to all of us the big round moon now shining brightly above. The animated state of the three in the back told Adrienne and I how happy they were, their exuberance had been topped up by those days of Florida sun, fun and togetherness.

The evening was calm and clear, and the night air was still warm as we began our drive to Miami.

There was little traffic and the car moved smoothly and quietly along the generally straight road.

Even the conversation was dwindling, and presently as we left the streetlights behind, all became quiet, and Adrienne confirmed that the children were asleep.

It was black, apart from occasional headlights and that huge full moon up there to my left outlining the sparse tall trees.

Adrienne thought she saw a reflection on water beyond the trees, but not long after, I sensed that she too was asleep. With three children she was always busy, but that day especially because we had all got up '*bright and early*' to enjoy our last day.

I saw the rear lights of a single-deck yellow bus in front of us, going quite slowly. Driving of course on the right-hand side of the road, I pulled out to the left to overtake. I had passed the front of the bus and had just returned to the nearside, when in my headlights I saw a big old rusty orange car without lights reversing at right angles, two car lengths in front of me from my left.

Adrienne and the children were all suddenly awake and aware of the danger. We all saw it at the same instant; there

71

was a shout of 'Look Out!' from Adrienne and from the back.

That biggest moment of my life caught in my headlights.

That tiny instant stays with me.

The fixed face of the driver, looking towards me, shocked.

His arm hanging loosely from his open window, with a can of drink in his hand.

It was too late.

I swerved to the right but caught the rear of his car with a crunching thud.

I woke up to an eerie silence; it seemed surreal, and strangely peaceful except for the sound of water coming into the car and getting louder. Dark, except for that big moon still on my left, its light glistening on the surface of the water.

Our car was floating upright on the surface of the Everglades.

In my groggy state the danger didn't register. I lay back. I saw and heard water coming in from below the windscreen in front of me and through the bottom of my door, which was, I think now, latched but slightly open.

No other noise.

I did nothing until Adrienne stirred me in a drowsy voice with, 'Close your door.' Incredibly I think I tried to do that. Then I remember nothing, until woken by cold water around me, in complete blackness and silence.

I panicked and thought of nothing but escape. If I'd heard, seen, or was touching somebody, I hope things would have been so different. As it was in that instant it was pure survival, and I thought only of escaping

Perhaps those words from Adrienne were still in my head,

or perhaps instinctively I put all my weight against the door, which was possibly still not quite closed. I put everything into one big push, and I was through. If that one push hadn't worked…, would I have become aware of the others? I don't know, but it has given me nightmares. It seemed a very long time before I reached light, and then the surface… and then the horror of where I was and who was below me. I shouted, but lights and help were far away. I tried to dive down, stretching my hands out but I touched nothing and saw nothing.

After what seemed ages but was probably minutes, I saw headlamps directed across the surface, and then there were two men in the water beside me. I shouted and kept shouting that my family was still down below, in the car.

I saw the blue emergency vehicle lights and brighter search-lights focused across the surface, and more people. Somebody grabbed hold of me, told me to calm down and pulled me to the side. It was a nightmare.

A woman on the bank drew me into her arms, and I buried my head hoping something that had happened so quickly had never happened at all. It just couldn't be. But I could hear and see the rescue workers a few feet away; this nightmare was real, and I was powerless.

All I loved were there. Something had to be done, but I couldn't do it. I looked, I pleaded, and I shouted as things were quietening down on the water.

I knew my family were all gone.

My beloved wife Adrienne, my darling boy Nigel, our beloved twins Anna-Jane and Lucy-Claire.

They were all innocent. They were all beautiful.

They were gone.

It was after midnight when I arrived, in my wet clothes, on a stretcher at the Baptist Hospital of Miami. I wasn't badly injured, just some teeth fractured on both sides, slivers of glass in my arm, and a very small dent in my forehead where I had hit the sun visor. I had been sedated in the ambulance and was in a numbed frenzy at the hospital.

Two male nurses attempted to calm me before the hospital duty manager arrived. It all seemed routine for him as he asked my name and then for my credit card. I hadn't got it because it was in the car. He thought for a moment then walked away. Minutes later he returned. He sympathised, he kept saying how sorry he was, but it was company policy that nobody could stay without a credit card. I would have to leave. He walked away.

The two male nurses were still there. One put his hand on my shoulder and said that *he* would make sure I could stay. 'Is there anyone I can contact?' he asked. I immediately thought of somebody at home, but I was in no state to recall numbers. I thought of British Airways at Miami Airport. He went away to ring them and was told they would call back.

Despite the hour, the call came: British Airways would indemnify all costs to the hospital. Only then was I moved from the reception area into a proper hospital bed and given drugs to send me to sleep. Due to my high state of tension, that didn't prove possible.

In the morning two men came in to see me. Local television had reported the accident saying that I was from Scotland and now recovering in the Baptist Hospital. These two had independently rung the hospital and asked if they could visit me; for absolutely no gain, just to chat and offer help. They lived in Miami but one of them was originally from Scotland and the other from Northern Ireland. They were priceless for me at that moment, two people on my side and by my side.

They were next to me when I was told the news that all my family had died. I'd hoped, and prayed, but now there was no hope, there wasn't anything. They had all been taken to the American Hospital in Miami after the rescuers had tried to resuscitate Nigel.

That was it; I had hoped for a miracle, but it hadn't come. I didn't want to believe it then and I still can't really believe it now.

I cried, I walked up and down, round and round endlessly, trying to cope with it.

If I stopped walking, it sank in, and I couldn't face that.

I got a telephone call to say that my British Airways boss at Gatwick, Captain Bill Brennen, was in the USA. He was preparing to fly down from New York and would be with me at the hospital the next day.

8

At some time during that awful first morning the Miami police arrived. In the state I was in, I couldn't have been much help to them, but their uniforms meant to me that somebody important had noticed. They would surely find out what happened and why.

Only two things they said remained with me after they left: the accident wasn't my fault, and they had the details of the other driver, who, they said, had state minimum insurance. They emphasised the state minimum insurance, but I wouldn't find out the significance till later. I never heard again from the Miami police.

A much-needed boost came with a telephone call from my father, my first conversation with anyone from home. Making a call abroad was not within his comfort zone at the best of times, so it really was wonderful.

My family had given me the best of times. This was the worst of times; my father was utterly overwhelmed, and I could hear my mother crying in the background, but they were trying hard to be as stoical as they could for my sake. Their call boosted me, but it emphasised the enormity of the tragedy and its effect on so many people, all suffering at that time.

When Captain Bill Brennan arrived, he was a great support. He listened patiently as I poured out my despair. Really listened. I could tell that, and it helped that my feelings were getting through to him. I knew he was there to help and straight away

I had confidence in him. I had only met him once before, and that was briefly at Gatwick. He was my boss, an ex-Fleet Air Arm pilot who was greatly respected, both as a pilot and manager. Though I didn't know him when he walked into the hospital, he immediately got my respect. I relied heavily on him for the next few weeks, and we became friends for life.

Bill wasn't the sort of man to pass by on the other side; he was there to help, and I couldn't have asked for anyone better. Step by step, overcoming my despair and my breakdowns, he carved a way forward. He said he would stay for as long as my family were there, the most reassuring words I could hear at that time.

I gave him details of friends and relations who needed to be told, though by that time it had been reported on TV at home, and I knew from my father's call that British Airways had contacted him. Bill would stay on, but when it was time for me to go back, he suggested a friend or relation should go with me.

My first thought was my elder brother, Colin, to whom I was always especially close.

I knew he would come, but he would need to get a passport, and the trip itself would be a real challenge for him. His presence would certainly have been reassuring.

But something in me said I should be making a gesture towards Adrienne's family; perhaps because I knew the devastation being wreaked in Sheffield at that moment. She was always the family favourite, and they would all be heartbroken. I wanted to talk to someone on her side of things; somebody who would be missing her as I was missing her. That's when I thought of exactly the right person: Adrienne's cousin, Alistair

M. He had a lifelong connection with Adrienne, they had the same birthday, and he was godfather to Nigel. And he was a lawyer.

It was an emotional and tearful moment on both sides when, two days later, Alistair walked into the hospital. Having him there, from Adrienne's side of the family, brought me a sense of closeness to her, and I was very pleased to see him. The mention of his mother Iris's name was enough to make me imagine the anguish she was feeling at that moment. Iris was like a mother to Adrienne and incredibly close to my children. Then Adrienne's sister Pat, then her brother… it was unending sadness being played out now back in the UK.

Alistair handled it all well as I told him how the accident had happened, and the situation as I understood it. Bill joined us and suggested a plan for the days ahead; Alistair and I would return to London the next morning and Bill would stay just long enough to arrange the return of my family, and then he would come back on the same flight. Alistair invited me to stay with him and his wife Sue in London for at least the first week after our return.

I had already received phone calls from Miami lawyers apparently anxious to represent me, and I got more while Alistair was with me. I had been in no mood to say anything to them, but for Alistair it was his line of business.

The question they all asked was, 'Did the other driver have state minimum insurance?', something that meant little to either of us, but which tallied with the words from the Miami policeman earlier.

Everything was going to be complicated, and Alistair offered to be my legal advisor throughout, an offer I was pleased to accept. He was a lawyer specialising in personal injury, albeit in the UK, but more than that, he was a very close relative and godfather to my son.

Letters arrived from strangers. One from a seventy-eight-year-old, who had 'lost many and seen a lot,' said, 'I'm sure there is a mission for you, something you will have to fulfil... don't disappoint your family by not taking an active part in life.' Another came from 'a grandmother in the USA' wishing me well. Those letters, like the visit from those two men on the first day, were of immense importance to me in the darkest of times.

Alistair and I arrived at Heathrow four days after the accident. I had been on sedatives for the journey, so not much was said. There was certainly a lot to think about, but not yet; my waking and sleeping thoughts were focused on the family I'd left behind in Florida.

Alistair's wife, Sue, met us at Heathrow and drove us to their house in North London. They had two very young daughters, but Sue had been moving things around so that I could stay. Within a very short time I got a reassuring call from my brother Colin. Bolstered by that, I phoned Alison and Ralph Risk, our close friends in Helensburgh, followed by Alistair's mother in Sheffield. My calls were short and sad, though I remember being uplifted by Ralph being typically sensible and positive when all around was gloom.

Alistair went off to his Chambers in Central London the next morning, leaving me with Sue and her children. Having been a nurse, as well as looking after her children, she very ably managed my sedatives and coped with my constant walking up and down the room. The tablets meant I was getting some sleep, and the pacing was a safety valve for my ever-growing tension. Whether awake or unevenly asleep, my family being still over in Florida made it all overpowering.

Alistair's wife Sue was a good nurse, and when we walked round the park with her young girls, a good listener. Urgent decisions had to be faced up to, and I talked them over with Alistair in the evenings. The mention of a funeral service numbed me but had to be discussed. Adrienne's beloved Sheffield was the obvious place for that with perhaps a memorial service in Helensburgh, where we had been living and had our happy family times.

Colin drove up from Maidstone. The second eldest in my family of six, and fourteen years older than me, I was desperate to see him. We were the closest in the family by a long way and in family battles he was always staunchly on my side. In grief I couldn't have done without him, from that very first meeting. My brain began to focus, and decisions were made.

Bill called from Miami and said that he would fly back with my family in three days' time, arriving at Heathrow at 11am on the Tuesday. He took in hand the arrangements at both Miami and Heathrow with the fine and thoughtful detail that he was so good at; what a help and relief that was.

A private room would be set aside at Heathrow, overlooking the gate where the aircraft carrying my family and Bill would dock. He had contacted the mortuary near Heathrow, ensuring that the awful scene due to be played out would go as smoothly as it possibly could.

I asked Colin to pass on these details to my family in Maidstone, as I wanted them all to be there. I remembered my wedding, where three of my siblings found an excuse not

80

to drive 'all that way' up to Sheffield. This time there could be no excuses, they *had* to be there; I'm sure their hearts were in the right place, but I knew that doing nothing, not interfering, was the default option for some of them.

On that cold February morning my entire Maidstone family gathered with me, awaiting the inbound flight from Miami.

Apart from Colin, it was the first time I had seen them since the accident. They looked pale and too shocked to say much. My mother was trying to hold back tears and my father seemed war worn.

The plane parked as we watched, and the passengers disembarked. One of them, Bill, walked around the plane to the door of the freight hold. My sister-in-law, Betty, clutched my hand tightly as the rear cargo door opened.

One by one the four coffins were taken carefully and slowly from the plane. I'm sure the sun did come out at that moment.

We watched in silence, completely numb, until long after everyone disappeared beneath us. It was Bill who stirred us. He gave a brief outline of what was to follow, then led Colin and myself down to the waiting car which would take us to the mortuary. Bill sat in the front seat for the twenty-minute journey, adding details to what he had said before; I was to officially identify each of my family, and we were limited to just thirty minutes. As we got out of the car, Colin clung tightly to me; I needed him there. Before we went through the mortuary doors I asked him to make absolutely sure I spent exactly the same time with each one.

Their heads were uncovered for us, and they looked almost as they had in life.

I saw Adrienne first. She looked serene, her blonde hair

curling over her forehead, which I leaned over and kissed. I said I loved her and I was sorry.

Then the girls. They looked almost unmarked, and still beautiful, except that Anna had a bruise on her forehead. I kissed them both in turn and said how much I loved them and that I knew they knew I loved them.

Then Nigel, my hero, and my hope in life. I kissed him, said I loved him and would always love him. And that I was sorry. With each of them not many words came, because as I looked, I hoped they knew what I wanted to say.

Colin tugged me and said it was time to go.

I went to Adrienne, my first love, the love of my life, and the reason why my family was so perfect. I gave her one very last kiss and my last words, 'I love you.'

I needed the supporting arms of Colin and Bill to get back to the car. Nothing was said on the journey because there was nothing to say.

We were driven back to Heathrow, and then Colin drove me to Alistair's house. There was much to think about, but nothing to say, and once more it was back to the only release that I knew, pacing up and down and round and around.

After a sedated night's sleep, it was back to walking, round the living room and then with Sue and her children in the park. Alistair was home, and there were decisions to be made. We came back to the funeral arrangements, which had to be confirmed.

First would be a memorial service at Old St Andrews Church in Colquhoun Square Helensburgh, where we often went as a family on Sunday mornings, and where we had all been four weeks before to see the girls receive their Church of Scotland hymn books. Then the funeral service two days later at Bents Green Methodist Church in Sheffield, where Adrienne and I had married fifteen years before.

Telephone calls went back and forth from Alistair's house in north London until dates were set for both. Alistair worked hard and my input was minimal other than to say yes or no, or to give names and addresses.

In the coming days I thought over specific things, such as hymns that I wanted, and I did speak to the vicars of both churches as the time drew near. I relied on lots of people in Sheffield and Helensburgh, at that time, especially Alistair and his family and the Risk family in Helensburgh.

I was especially grateful to them, but I'm sure their motivation was Adrienne and the children, because I saw their love shine through. That love drove all of us at that difficult time, because for them, things had to go perfectly, nothing less would do.

Days later it was time to go to Scotland. Colin would be my constant companion for the trials ahead. He met me at Heathrow to catch the shuttle to Glasgow.

9

The gloomy cold grey day that met us at Glasgow Airport matched our mood exactly.

Almost the same bleak wintry cold of that early morning just two weeks ago when we'd excitedly left the staff car park for a holiday in Barbados. We were too full of excitement then to worry about the hour or the cold as we scampered, suitcases and children in hand, across to the terminal.

Two weeks later our red Audi was there, as we'd left it, looking snowbound and solitary in an almost empty car park. Parked close by and waiting to meet us was my indispensable friend Ralph Risk, fully prepared with the spare key he'd collected from my house and jump-leads in case the battery was flat. Seeing him was wonderful, a return to a small part of my family life.

But the car brought fear. Inside was an undisturbed snapshot of life as it was. This would be difficult. Seeing the blanket on the back seat that had warmed the children on that early morning drive to the airport was an instant shock. For a while it overwhelmed me. I remembered Adrienne running upstairs to fetch it when she realised the air was so cold.

Once again, I needed a sympathetic but bolstering 'Come on Al' from Colin as ever just behind me. For the past few hours I'd been anxious to get things moving, but now real-life was all around me and things couldn't be hurried.

Colin drove us to Ralph's house in Helensburgh. The old

stone house had been a sort of second home for my family over the past seven years, with Adrienne and Ralph's wife Alison becoming very close friends. All six children from our two families went to Hermitage Primary School and were of a similar age.

Now I walked into a very different home, sad and subdued with all of us still in shock and trying hard to keep emotions under control.

Ralph Risk was ideal for any catastrophe, always intelligent, measured and calm, and I was thankful to have him in Helensburgh where there were so many loose ends. He came from a large, long-living and clever family (his brother was Governor of the Bank of Scotland), and he loved Adrienne and my family.

Ralph had organised the following day's memorial service and ran through the details. He even knew the weather forecast, which thankfully was fine but cold. The service had been brought forward, ahead of the funeral service, to try and draw a line as soon as possible under the grief now pervading the children's school. The broad details had already been sent to the local newspaper, to the school and to the many people who wanted to come.

We had to talk about my house, just up the road in Upper Colquhoun Street, because it was sold and soon it had to be emptied for the new owners. Ralph said he would organise that in good time and put everything in store. Without Ralph Risk, like Bill Brennen and my brother Colin, an awful situation would have been even worse.

The next morning dawned as forecast, cold but sunny, with traces of snow on the ground. To pass the time and try to ease the tensions, Colin and I drove into Glen Fruin, the long valley behind Helensburgh, and our favourite place for walks and picnics. Even those hills that had seen so many things over so many years, seemed sad.

Old St Andrew's Church looked majestic in the sunshine. As we walked from the car I saw people making their way towards the big oak side doors, both young and old, some disabled and in wheelchairs. I saw children in school uniform, familiar parents and teachers, and members of the swimming club. The Cubmaster in uniform alongside the Brown Owl from the girls' Brownies, and Mrs Kelso, the children's piano teacher. Getting closer I recognised some of the children in wheelchairs and their parents from Glasgow. Little was said, but I was lifted by the support I felt. I knew that Adrienne and the children had reached the hearts of so many people in Helensburgh and beyond, and now I could see that in the eyes of so many faces.

We were met by Minister David Reid, and led through the arched wooden doors, where we'd all walked for Sunday service four weeks before. The church felt familiar, bright, warm, and welcoming.

The first hymn I'd chosen was *All Things Bright and Beautiful* which I thought summed up my family. The hymns were loud, and the service was beautiful, all of which gave me the strength to stand there as my mind wandered inevitably between the present and the past in a bit of a blur.

The words from the minister were of comfort, as he tried to put some context around what had happened. I'd chosen the hymn *God is Working His Purpose Out* because I liked the tune and I sort of wished for the sentiment behind it. But something

I could never accept, because there could never be an adequate purpose for what had happened.

Though I was never a devout Christian, and shunned rituals of most kinds, the rousing hymns, the thoughtful and kind words from the minister and perhaps our association with that big old church, were a great support to me. In the past few days I had often put my hand up to heaven and shaken my fist. But that service, the words spoken, and the numbers of people there, gave me at least the beginnings of calm.

I left the church with Colin, pleased to recognise people in the congregation but in no mood to talk. We sat in the car for a few minutes, both of us trying to take everything in.

My house was just five minutes away, and it seemed right to drive back there now, to reconnect with my family and to where we belonged. The keys were still in the glove box where they'd been placed fifteen days before.

Firlands looked lovely in the last light of a winter's afternoon. Light snow framed the tall fir trees to the side and the small stone wall I'd painstakingly built to the front. I felt mocked by the For Sale notice, still standing outside even though the house was sold. Without the sale we wouldn't have been in Florida.

Our front door was a shade of green that Adrienne and I had spent hours choosing. I unlocked it with the same mix of fear and elation that I'd felt as I unlocked our car in the staff car park the day before. It felt comforting to step into the hall, half-expecting the children to run down the stairs or come in from the kitchen. With each step reality crept in, the euphoria disappeared and I was in tears.

I didn't go in to the kitchen, instead I headed up the stairs, instantly beckoned by the children's bedrooms. On Lucy's bed I saw the big fluffy Paddington Bear with his brown duffel coat and bright red Wellington boots. Another bear in typically more subdued and coordinated colours sat on Anna's bed. Gifts they'd loved from the Christmas just gone.

It was getting too difficult, and it was time to leave. I closed my eyes to say something to Nigel in his room, and left. On the way I picked up the two furry toys.

That night I paced around the Risk's house before tablets got me to sleep. Colin and I set off next morning for Sheffield, calling briefly to see Peter and Yvonne who were still looking after our dog Sophie. They were friends since RAF days, and we had followed them to Chesham where we bought our first house, and then to Helensburgh. Yvonne was one of Adrienne's closest friends, and patiently taught the girls to horse ride on Sunday afternoons. It was an emotional meeting, not least with Sophie, and I promised to collect her in the coming weeks.

The journey down to Sheffield was full of thoughts from the day before, and the day just ahead. I sat in the passenger seat, kept going by a mixture of adrenalin and fitful sleep, reinforced as necessary by words of encouragement from Colin. It must have seemed a long drive for him, emotionally drained as he was. It was good to reach the city.

Meeting Iris for the first time since the accident was always going to be painful, because she was perhaps the one person who loved Adrienne and the children as much as I did. We had spent Christmas with her, just two months before.

We'd spoken on the phone, but as I approached her house, my overwhelming sadness was tinged with a sense of guilt now that I was in Adrienne's part of the world. My fault or not, I was the cause of terrible grief in their lives.

We met with tears in our eyes. To Adrienne, to me and to our children Iris was as good as it got. Like Adrienne, she was elegant and sensible with a clear sense of right and wrong. Like Adrienne she was Yorkshire to the core. Despite all the traumas and all the sadness, she had worked tirelessly, helped by Alistair, to organise the funeral service, now in two days time. Tomorrow would be busy.

With Colin by my side as usual, now as a sounding board as much as a source of encouragement, I began by meeting the vicar of Bents Green Methodist Church to discuss the service. Although he wasn't the vicar who married us, I was comforted to hear that he knew Adrienne and her family well. Lots of local people had been in touch with him, wanting to be at the service, including ladies from Silver Hill Dairies where Adrienne had worked as a young girl on Saturday mornings. That delighted me, but once again brought home the enormity of it all.

I telephoned John Heath, the Sheffield undertakers, and was asked if I would like to see my family for one last time. Of course, I would.

Adrienne's brother Howard came with us, and we arrived in the late afternoon at the mortuary on the outskirts of Sheffield. I had with me the two Paddington Bear toys I had brought down from Helensburgh, and we were met by one of the Heath brothers.

It was a numbing moment for the three of us as we walked in. As before, I asked Colin to ensure that I spent exactly the same time with each of them.

This time just a small piece of each face was visible, but very recognisable and very beautiful. As before, I went first to Adrienne, then the girls and then Nigel. Just a few words to each, while looking and thinking and crying. And despairing because this was final. Just before leaving I tucked the Paddington Bear toys into the girls' coffins, before giving my very last kiss to Adrienne.

All three of us hung tightly together as we left, completely shattered. The undertaker asked how I wanted the burials arranged in the double plot in Ecclesall churchyard. I said it should be Adrienne first, then the two girls next to each other, then Nigel above. I got peace from thinking that one day I would lie next to Nigel and close to Adrienne and the girls.

Iris's house was full but unsurprisingly very quiet when we got back. My sister-in-law Sonia suggested that I might like to walk down to her house that evening. I went with Colin and Howard and accepted the offer of a small beer, my first alcohol for weeks. It was either the stress or the sedatives, but after a couple of sips I was sick all over the carpet.

That next day, the big day, was thankfully cold but sunny. Snow was still quite thick on the ground. My teeth either side that had been damaged in the accident had caused no problems until then, but now I had toothache.

I started my usual habit of pacing around the house. Alistair suggested we should go for a drive in to Derbyshire, stopping at a dentist that Iris knew on the way. They kindly sorted my toothache, then Alistair and I drove across the Yorkshire border in to Derbyshire, aimlessly and without conversation but passing a couple of hours.

Alistair timed our arrival back at his mother's house perfectly, so there was little time to spare and people were already gathering around the church. A local newspaper photographer was waiting at the gate, and Howard rushed out of the house to usher him away. Thirty minutes later Alistair and I joined Colin and relatives in the hallway, ready to leave.

The sun shone brightly, though it was cold. Outside the church, exactly where most of our wedding photos had been taken fifteen years before, I nodded to my mother and father, brothers and sister as they walked in.

The two black hearses were soon there, and the four coffins carried forward. As they passed I leant forward and kissed each one.

At that moment I sensed someone sidling up behind me and a hand on my shoulder. The hand clenched my shoulder and a voice whispered, 'Stand firm, Alan'. It was my aged Auntie Frances, a schoolfriend of my mother from Edinburgh and for years a loved friend of mine. I wonder if she could ever realise how important those words were to me at that moment and in the years ahead.

As in Scotland, the church was full, the lighting bright and the hymns I had chosen were as rousing as they could be. 'All Things Bright and Beautiful' was again the first, because the children loved it and it summed them all up. I'm sure the service was beautiful, but for me it was truthfully but a blur in the background as my eyes went from coffin to coffin, talking to each in turn. I did hear and remember the very personal and heartfelt words spoken by the minister. Those words bolstered me, as did the singing, the numbers of people there and the love they showed towards Adrienne and the children.

We filed out the church, the service over. Minutes later we

all stood in absolute silence outside the old gates of Ecclesall churchyard, before following the four coffins on the long snow-covered path, everybody in their own thoughts.

As we turned a corner, I glimpsed the long snake of people trailing behind. Then the final moment of all.

As each coffin was lowered, I said their names out loud; Adrienne, Anna-Jane, Lucy-Claire, Nigel.

Then silence.

It was real and it was final.

My lowest point in life, and there was nothing to say.

We all stood thinking.

It was over.

All there were shaken, distressed and saddened, but most would go back to their own lives and succeed in pushing it all into the background, albeit perhaps with a lifelong scar.

As others filed away, Colin and I stayed for a while, just looking and thinking. I had one overriding thought. Whatever my suffering, however I felt, it was nothing compared to what they went through that night at the Everglades. I would never forget that.

A quiet voice from the vicar encouraged us to go back to the car. If God really was working His purpose out, I would take some persuading.

10

I ris's house was full, mostly with relatives from both sides of the family, but also with some old friends that I recognized from the RAF and from school, including schoolfriends John Chrystal who had come especially from Connecticut, and Robin Murray. It helped to see them there. The drinks and food were generally sidelined, overtaken by the shock of witnessing the funeral of four precious young people.

I received sympathy and support from everybody, but here, amongst Adrienne's family in Sheffield I felt that I had let them down. Although not my fault, (and nobody ever asked for details), the bottom line was that I had come into Adrienne's life and taken her away forever, and my presence or survival was perhaps to them little compensation. I might have been over-sensitive, but that is what I sensed then and over the months and years to come, and perhaps what I should have expected. That day was always going to be one to endure. I coped with my usual walking up and down but was pleased to go to bed with a sleeping tablet.

I travelled down to London with Alistair, and he suggested that I stay at his house for at least another week. He returned to work, leaving early the next morning, and I returned to my previous routine of pacing around the floor, only stopping to eat or sleep or take a walk with Sue and the children in the park. There were many things to sort out but they would have to wait.

Since the accident I had been desperate to have some photos of my family, and Ralph Risk up in Helensburgh promised to go to my house and choose some to send down to me. After a week I phoned Ralph to remind him, but they had been sent days before. Alistair had forgotten that a quite large cardboard box had arrived and was in the basement.

Unfortunately, the basement was cold and wet, so the cardboard box and some of the photos inside were damaged. Alistair was working hard, both at his chambers in London and at coping with my problems at home, so I understood that perhaps he'd forgotten the delivery. It was the absence of an apology or even an understanding as to why it was so important to me that I found disappointing, and that was the first wedge in our always arms-length relationship.

At about that time British Airways made the generous offer to provide counselling, and as with just about everything in those first weeks, I discussed it with Alistair. To his credit he was forever stable, and I certainly wasn't. Counselling was relatively rare in those days, and I was persuaded by Alistair that things were complicated enough, with having to find a house, return to my job and a myriad of other things to sort out. I decided that another voice would just muddy the waters, so I turned down the offer.

It was twenty years before I found out, in a secluded, wooden shack overlooking Haut Bay near Cape Town, how useful good trauma counselling could be. It definitely would have helped me at that time and perhaps could have changed my life.

Wrong, instant decisions were inevitable as we tried to make headway in difficult circumstances. Alistair was there for me in those initial two or three weeks. He helped as he thought best at a time when everybody was under pressure, and he took the lead when my mind was fogged. Providing a base for me when I literally didn't have one was something I would always be grateful for, but now I sensed it was time to give Alistair and Sue their house back.

I talked my options over with Colin and, as I thought, my mother and father expected me to move back to the family house I had left nineteen years before. It was natural and kind of them, but I couldn't do it. The accident, apart from the horror, had brought me back almost to square one. Returning 'home' would, in my mind, complete that fall.

Colin listened to all that and told me he had already talked it over with his wife, Jill. They were happy for me to move into their house in Maidstone for a few weeks, near to where the rest of my family lived, including my mother and father. It was a brave as well as a generous offer to make. I was having deep bouts of depression and they had a small house and two young children. But I knew the offer was sincere and I was pleased, and relieved to accept.

In my last few days at Alistair's house, the name of a Miami lawyer called Rentz was mentioned. He had somehow contacted Alistair and was apparently 'handling' Mr. Anderson's state minimum $20,000 third-party car insurance policy. I never understood how or why, but Mr. Rentz was later described as 'my lawyer' when we returned to Miami. I cannot recall ever meeting him or receiving any of that $20,000, so I assume that somebody used it to pay hospital bills and for the flights home, after the usual lawyer's deduction of 40%.

I left Alistair's house extremely grateful to him and Sue for letting me stay at a vital time. Over that last week, and with those walks in the park, I began to feel better, in that I took less sedation and was thinking more clearly. The incident with the photographs gave me the necessary jolt to cast off from others and think for myself. Except that is, in legal matters, where I was still grateful to take the lead from Alistair.

Anna-Jane and Lucy-Claire. First day at school!

Part three

Two girls in silk kimonos, both beautiful

11

Colin and Jill's three bedroomed semi-detached house in Aylesford near Maidstone, was close to my parents and to the rest of my family. It was a squeeze to fit me in, because they had two young children, Diane and Andrew, and it wasn't a big house, but they all made me very welcome.

I wasn't the best of guests, because I was still on a knife-edge between coping and not, and needed my pacing up and down as well as sedatives from the local doctor, but Jill and Colin were easy to be with and good and sensible listeners. Colin would do anything for me, and even at work, would come home if asked. For a while I enjoyed the new calmness after the dramas of the past weeks, though many things were hanging in the air, and decisions now being asked for.

Alistair had received frequent letters and calls from Miami lawyers, anxious to represent my interests (and their interests) in a civil case for potentially large damages. In a sense, compensation seemed tacky; losing my family and replacing them with money. What *did* interest me, and I'd heard nothing more about it, was simple; what had happened that night, and how was the investigation going? It seemed clear cut; a car had reversed without lights directly in front of us on a dark road, and the driver had a can of drink in his hand. That single act caused the loss of my wife and my three children, so surely *something* had to be happening, and by now I should have heard from the Miami police as part of an investigation?

I found out thirty-five years later that the Miami Police Department did make one attempt to get in touch, in a strangely roundabout way. I now know that on the 10 April, exactly three weeks after the accident, my father received a phone call from British Airways. He meticulously wrote down everything that was said. The police were using British Airways as my forwarding address rather than that of my father, who I'd given as my next of kin. In such a serious case, didn't basic humanity demand that I be spoken to directly? Or be asked to call them back to a given number?

The police message said:

An Accident Report has been submitted to the Dade County State Attorney's Office in Miami, for a decision on prosecution. If they decide not to prosecute, responsibility will be with Atkinson to initiate civil charges. For this he will need a Florida lawyer.

After saying they could suggest a lawyer, the message went on: *The police report will be available in a week's time for the cost of $25.*

The coldness of that message, the way it was relayed via my employers rather than directly to me or my father, and even its closing advertisement for a lawyer, mirrors the same ice-cold behaviour that I'd experienced at the Baptist hospital on the night of the accident.

My father says at the bottom of his written note: *Gave the message to Ralph Risk in Scotland.*

Sadly, it didn't reach me for thirty-five years, though I suspect it was sent to Alistair, who I was to find out had a different view of a prosecution. If he had received it three weeks after the accident, if it had an address and telephone number attached... what a difference that would have made. I cannot imagine that the police in the UK, after an accident which killed four people, relaying a message via somebody's employer.

Getting justice in the USA wasn't going to be easy. The phrase 'state minimum insurance' kept cropping up and was obviously relevant, but I didn't know why.

I met with Alistair to discuss the whole legal situation. He repeated his offer to be my volunteer legal advisor and went further, saying he wanted all legal correspondence from and to Miami to go through him. I was grateful as well as relieved, because it was getting complicated. American Law was different, I could see that already, but Alistair seemed the ideal man for the job, as both a successful lawyer and a specialist in personal injury law. And he was a close relative, so I felt lucky.

My paramount interest was for a proper prosecution of Anderson, to ask what happened that night and what was in that can of drink. This was not shared by Alistair and that struck me as odd. Time and time again he brushed aside my concerns saying, 'The law will take its course.'

Having heard nothing from the Miami police, I was beginning to have doubts, thinking that nothing could take its course unless I, the main witness, was asked questions. I wanted a clear and loud acknowledgment that something very wrong happened that night, and I wanted it soon. To brush what happened aside, even to put it on the back burner, was inhumane as well as unjust.

With the complications that were already beginning to surface, I offered to pay for all of Alistair's work on my case, but he swiftly rejected that with a wave of his hand. He was very pleased to look after my legal interests for nothing. That meant the civil case, because Alistair just didn't want to get involved in a prosecution, though it wasn't until we got to Miami a couple of years later that he explained why. It was the civil case for him, and he finished up by saying we should both go to Miami sooner rather than later, to appoint an American lawyer. He would produce a shortlist from those who had already been in touch.

Now I was clearly on my own with the prosecution and, each day of silence from Miami built up the tension. Needing to know what was happening, I phoned the Miami Police Department, the district attorneys, even Ralph Nader, the American consumer rights specialist, or anyone else who I thought might help. I always chose a bright sunny day, because it was too depressing at other times, and I received promises, interest and annoying disinterest, and I was passed from pillar to post, but nobody had any significant information they could lay their hands on. I found out that Miami was a very big place, and I didn't know exactly where it had all happened.

Up until now, I had been swept along on a predetermined path, centred around the funeral service and bolstered by adrenalin and sedatives. Now there were new urgent things to think about, and it all seemed overwhelming as I paced up and down. Colin would do anything I asked, and Jill was forever patient, but generally my family found my situation equally overwhelming.

I needed to talk things through with someone; I was now a stone's throw from the rest of my family, but sadly they were willing but not able to help. Adrienne's more worldly family in Sheffield, on the other hand, I knew were able, but, for the moment anyway, didn't seem very willing. I think they were exhausted mentally and physically by the past weeks, and, quite truthfully like most people now just wanted to put sadness away and get on with their lives.

A saviour came in the form of David, my sister Pauline's husband. He, I think, saw the void in my life and began to call me or visit me every day, which was just what I needed. I still paced the floor and had very low points, but Jill, Colin and now David gradually got me to a state where I could face the world.

Decisions were being demanded, starting with my house buyers in Helensburgh, who wanted to know when they could move in, but the house had first to be emptied and the contents put in to store. It was a difficult job at any time but now with everything exactly as we had left it that February morning, it would be intensely emotional. Ralph Risk and his friend, (and ours), Jimmy Cook bravely took on the task, and within a week Firlands was empty and everything in store in Glasgow. A terrific task, very thoughtfully and carefully done. It was good to know that most of the toys were given to the children's friends, and especially pleasing that Nigel's prized blue *Chopper* bike was given to his friend Mark. Virtually everything else went into store, though special things found their way down to me, such as the cub and brownie uniforms and the girl's riding hats. Things I could never let go of.

The owners of Downsway, my dream house in Steyning wanted to know when I would move in. The contract was signed; and the divorcing couple were desperate to get my money and move out. A few weeks ago, I had been counting the hours to moving in, but now, because of everything, I had doubts. I didn't know how I would feel; could I live in that house without them? I had to see it again.

Jill and I drove down to Steyning. The house enticed me

as before, sitting beautifully on top of the hill, but this time I didn't have Adrienne and the children standing enthusiastically next to me. I felt weak as I walked to the front door; it had been the centre of my dreams for months. I knew it was perfect, and yet now it was linked to all that had gone wrong.

I actually started to walk away with my mind made up, till a tug and, 'Come on Al' from Jill got me moving, and I knocked on the oak door. It brought the woman I'd met months before, still getting divorced and now desperate for me to complete the deal. I walked in, thinking, 'Why not?' because I *did* need a house, and I still loved it.

Upstairs things changed. I pointed out the room where Lucy had decided to sleep, and then 'Anna's room'. Jill started crying and said the house had too many memories, and if I bought it, she could never visit me. In my fragile state, those words backed up what I'd already been half-thinking, so I pulled out of my dream house there and then.

I never knew if that was the right decision, perhaps a counsellor would have helped. I did later learn that it can help to cope with the past if you live with the past, so perhaps it was a decision taken too quickly.

Four years later I did a hang-gliding course off the hill not far from the house, and one day I ventured towards it, but the front gate was the closest I wanted to go. (Bizarrely a house I never owned played a recurring part in my life. Forty years on, my new doctor lives in that same house. He invited me round for a drink, but I decided I wasn't brave enough; perhaps I should have lived with the past.)

Back at Colin's house it was good to have one decision made, though to lose something else that I really wanted felt like yet another defeat. A slight consolation was that a family house big enough for five would be difficult to look after.

My mind was never far from the graveyard in Sheffield, and I was pleased to get a call from Mr. Corker, the Sheffield stonemason working on the new gravestone. I'd chosen a simple yet appropriate stone, and now he needed to know the words I'd chosen.

They had to be simple but adequate too. The date of the accident; 17 February 1981, followed by the four names, one underneath the other; Adrienne Claire, Anna-Jane, Lucy-Claire, Nigel James. At the bottom, very simply, *My loved and loving family.* Nothing more. Nothing less. Though I did ensure that there would be space for my name, under Nigel's, for when the time comes.

The sixth member of my family was Sophie, our King Charles Cavalier dog, and she was still being looked after by friends Peter and Yvonne in Helensburgh. It was time to collect her, and, at the same time retrieve the MGB that I'd bought as a surprise birthday present for Adrienne two years before. It was now occupying space in Ralph Risk's garage. I felt low, so seeing the Risks and collecting Sophie would cheer me up.

I flew to Glasgow, and Ralph picked me up from the airport. It was not long since the memorial service, and as bright as Ralph and Alison always were, it was difficult not to feel and see the sadness, especially in the eyes of their children. I realised I'd come back too soon, things were still too raw and I was a reminder of all things just past. As much as they made me very welcome, (and Ralph had cleaned the MGB, filled it with petrol, and it sat there gleaming outside his garage), I decided to head off south next morning.

After selecting a couple of the pot plants that Ralph had retrieved from clearing my house, and carefully placing them in the footwell, I set off on the journey south, looking forward to collecting Sophie. She and I hadn't always seen eye to eye, but from now on we would be soul mates, and I hurried to the door of Yvonne and Peter, her custodians for the last few weeks.

Sophie rushed down the hallway, I'm sure looking past me for Adrienne and the children, till she decided I was a good second-best. Emotions overflowed everywhere, not just with Sophie, because Peter and Yvonne had watched our family grow since we were in the RAF together. Everybody had red eyes and thoughts of much happier times and my emotional reunion with Sophie surprised me and probably her.

With Sophie ensconced in the navigator's basket and pot plants waving around her ears, we set off in the MGB on our journey together. We meandered down the A1, in no particular hurry, and to be truthful, with no particular place to go. Sophie and I had a lot to catch up on.

She settled quickly into Colin's house and enjoyed all the attention she was now given as the fifth member of their family. Unfortunately, the visit back to Scotland and even being reunited with Sophie put me back into my non-sleeping mode. Even my walks around the park with Jill didn't calm me, because although recounting my family stories to her was cathartic up to a point, there was something missing. Jill was patient and sympathetic, but she had only known Adrienne and the children from a distance, having met them just once or twice a year. I could say, and kept saying, that they were wonderful, but I was surrounded by people who hadn't really known them. That was the big downside of having to move south immediately after the accident.

I started having vivid dreams that one of the children had survived, waking up convinced it was true. The thought gave me such comfort that sometimes it would lodge at the back of my mind for days. What a difference it would have made if just one of my family had survived. This thought led on to me wondering how Adrienne would have coped in my place. Much better, I was sure, and I guessed she would have returned to the Risks' house in Helensburgh before permanently moving to her close and worldly-wise relations in Sheffield. But me, I was in no man's land.

In desperation I started going to church, and I persuaded Jill to come with me. Different churches, because I think we tried them all, in a wide circle around Maidstone. One Sunday evening we found ourselves in what seemed to be a very 'high' church from the moment we walked in. It was dark, with a steeply pitched ceiling and pews similarly highly angled towards the heavens. The smell of the incense, the fogginess and the odd tinkle of bells in the background made us wonder what we were letting ourselves in for, and we instinctively aimed for seats at the back, and in the far corner.

The vicar walked in; very tall, dressed in black from head to toe, and with a long black beard. He looked very Greek, very foreboding, and to me every inch like Archbishop Makarios, President of Cyprus in the sixties and seventies. His eyes fixed on us, probably as newcomers, and he made his way to the back of the church before sidling along to where we were sat, us watching his every move.

He leaned down and in a very deep cockney voice, he said, 'If all this gets a bit 'ot for you mate, I should go out after the second 'ymn'. We were surprised, relieved but impressed, and stayed until the very end.

That was light relief, but the church visits did serve a purpose, because they gave me a time and a place to focus on my family. I got into a rhythm (which I still do today) of picking out four items around the altar and linking each to one of my family. I close my eyes and say the Lord's Prayer. Then looking at the items in turn, I say something to each of them.

Those were difficult times. 'Stand Firm', those words whispered to me at the funeral, became increasingly important. It seemed as if something was happening every day to make matters worse, though it probably wasn't.

I was in a downward spiral, and once or twice Jill was so worried that she called Colin home from work to calm me. I sensed, and I think they sensed as well, that things were in the balance.

Keeping active calmed me down. I had already walked miles on the carpets of Sheffield, London, and now Maidstone. Exercise, even pacing up and down the carpet, seemed to put my mind in order, and that may simply have been because some of my thoughts were focused on where I was going. Pacing up and down diverted my mind, made me see things in the round, and sort of wiped the slate clean. When I did sit down, I was calmer, and generally more able to see the wood for the trees.

So began what I called, my 'diversionary tactics'. I created boxes in my mind, in which I put things *till later*. The *till later* part was the important thing; there was always a box for my family, set aside *till later*, when I could be by myself with my thoughts, my photos and (especially when I had a house), my music. Thoughts of the family were never far away but I tried to deflect them, *till later.* These tactics crept in bit by bit and didn't always work, but allowed me, I think, to generally move forward.

The vicar who had conducted the funeral had given me a small book, *The Prophet* by Kahlil Gibran. He'd written some encouraging words on the title page, but now, for the first time I read beyond and was surprised. I saw words that were thought provoking, but at the same time immensely soothing, and for the next few months *The Prophet,* alongside my music and visits to Sheffield were the mental medicines I needed. (Many years later, my neighbour in North Yorkshire was diagnosed with terminal cancer. I gave her my copy of *The Prophet,* and it helped her so much that she included a passage in her self-scripted funeral service.)

Not being around people who *could* help me, (as opposed to people who *wanted* to help me), forced me into a *putting into boxes* habit, so that I could concentrate on the present. Together with reading the odd chapter from *The Prophet* and moments alone with my music I felt stronger and began look-ing forward as well as backward. People looked at me sadly and didn't mention my family, but instead of letting that create a depressing void in me I looked ahead to when that would change. I'd look forward to my next trip to Sheffield and my visit to Iris when we would talk about them, in sadness and happiness at the same time, sitting on her sofa with gin and tonics in hand. Sheffield was now my place of escape.

I thought I was now, for the first time, on top of things. and I was certainly sleeping better. Bill Brennan kept in touch and noticed the change. He mooted the idea of returning to work, initially in the office until I was passed medically fit to fly. I hesitated for a day or two, wondering if my moments of melancholy would be best out of the public gaze. Then I accepted Bill's offer, deciding I should return to the outside world and meet people who knew nothing of my trauma. Hopefully I would feel more normal and less of a survivor.

Just six weeks after the accident I began work in the British Airtours offices at Gatwick airport. I was doing mundane things, but that didn't matter because I was once more putting on my uniform and leaving the house in the morning. I had rejoined the world. Yet again, I was grateful for the input of Captain Bill Brennen.

Ten days later, after a very thorough medical check, where the emphasis, quite reasonably was on my mental state, I was declared 'fit to fly'. A couple of days later I was airborne again, watching from the third pilot's seat behind the two pilots. Then it was one step forward, literally, because for my next flight I was back in the co-pilot's seat, albeit with a 'safety-pilot' sitting behind watching. As I sat in the seat my mind did wander, back to the last time I was there with my family at home, but I couldn't dwell long in the past because there were checks to be done, radio calls to make, and my mind was hauled back to the present.

The fourth of April 1981 was my first unsupervised flight, and a big step forward that *had* to go well for my future's sake. It was a fairly short flight, to Milan and back, and it wasn't until we climbed away from Milan Linate airport on the way back that I actually touched the controls for the first time. But it did go well, it was good to be flying again, and I looked upwards and onwards, in all ways.

12

Flying immediately brought direction back into my life. The discipline, the uniform, the checking-in, the flight preparation and then the flying, all focused my mind away from what I was tempted to think about. At work especially, I kept my emotions and some of my thoughts to myself, much as I had done growing up and trying to do homework in a family that didn't believe in homework.

Work was now my way forward, so indispensable, that I daren't make a mistake for fear of everything tumbling down. I was always shy and not good in large company, but now I was especially careful to keep control, not saying too much and certainly not drinking too much. It suited me that colleagues who knew what had happened just gave sympathetic looks, because they didn't know what to say. It was the, 'I don't know how you can stand up', that always stumped me however many times I heard it. It was chillingly negative, and I suppose there was no answer, except that hearing those words made it less likely that I would be able to stand up. Sometimes I didn't really know how myself, but the only alternative was to lie down and give up, and my wife, my children and myself were the three reasons, helped by my essential anchors, who at that time were my brother Colin, my brother-in-law David and Bill Brennen, my boss at Gatwick. I never came close to that.

A couple of weeks after that 'first' flight was 18 April, my twin daughters' ninth birthday and the day excited me as it always did. I would go up to the graveside to mark it, and in a way celebrate it, before spending the night with Iris. We would have dinner in Hathersage at the Chequers Inn and talk of them all, but on that night, especially the girls. Before that I had three more flights, and as well as the date, the prospect of going back to Sheffield for the first time since the funeral started to weigh me down. My last flight before the eighteenth was a long one, to Rhodes and back, and I sat in the car afterwards for a considerable time, exhausted emotionally far more than physically. I stayed there until I regained my equilibrium, pleased that I now had two weeks holiday to recover and regroup.

The eighteenth was thankfully going to be a bright spring day, and I set off early from Colin's house. I felt as I had on those flights from Bahrain to see Adrienne, when every minute got me closer to where I really wanted to be.

It was my first visit to Ecclesall churchyard since the funeral, and I parked right outside the churchyard gates, where the cortege had been just weeks before. I set off from the car with a large bunch of daffodils, and two red roses. The long path took me under big old trees, past gravestones large and small, upright and crumbling that I hadn't noticed before, but would soon become old friends. The path turned sharply, there were no overhanging trees, so the sun shone brightly. Children's voices came from the school playground on my right which bordered the graveyard, and where Adrienne had been taught as an infant.

There was the grave, our grave, next to the path and under a newly planted tree. Stark, that's how it felt, both what I could see and the reality I felt. The new headstone was bright gleaming white and showed the words exactly as I'd asked. I filled the metal vase from a tap I noticed up there towards the school and added my daffodils which I dedicated to each in turn. The roses on their special day were for my darling twin girls. That felt good, and I was close to them, until reality and the futility that went with it punched home. Somebody walked past and asked if I was all right. I said I was, but there was no way that I could be. I stayed for a long time.

It was fortunate that Iris's house was a short drive away, and our meeting was always going to be highly emotional for us both. We hadn't met since the funeral, and for the very first time it was just the two of us. As the two who were closest to my wife and children, we had a lot to talk about. The photos around the room stirred memories that meant everything to us, and at last I could share those thoughts with somebody who really knew them almost as I did. That was the big downside of moving south from Scotland immediately after the accident.

With the birthday over, calm returned and I went back to the busy summer flying schedules at Gatwick, as well as looking for a house to buy. Hearing nothing from Miami, I arranged a meeting with the MP for the Maidstone area, John Stanley. He listened carefully, agreed that I should have heard from the Miami police, would 'chase it up' and would get back to me.

As the summer wore on, and with Alistair still too busy to go to Miami I wondered, and not for the first time, if I'd made a big mistake in agreeing to an unpaid legal advisor. His oft repeated, 'the law will take its course' was starting to ring hollow, not helped by the reply from my MP. John Stanley who forwarded a letter from Lord Trefgarne at the Foreign Office that said nothing specific about my case but more or less

112

repeated the same phrase Alistair used. My instinct was that, if the law was taking its course, eight months without hearing anything about such a serious accident meant it was making very slow progress.

When the busy holiday flying schedules from Gatwick were slowing down and, after hearing from Alistair that a visit to Miami was due 'any time soon', I thought it was time for a change of scene.

My school friend John Chrystal lived in the USA and had flown over for the funeral. An invitation to his wedding in October in Connecticut went over my head at the time, and I hadn't said yes or no. Now, seven months later, was the time to say yes.

I flew with Laker Airways on their new Skytrain service from Gatwick to New York, where John collected me and drove us northwards to his sprawling timbered house in Ridgefield, Connecticut.

Everything was big, from the refrigerator in the kitchen to the massive new IBM mainframe 360 computer that just about filled one room. I met his beautiful Swedish wife-to-be, Elisabeth, for the first time, and when I looked at her, his house, his car and later his boat, he was a very different John Chrystal from the one I sat next to at school. It was a second coming rather than a change.

Back then he was a good athlete, but not especially attractive to girls, which made me look relatively good and was possibly one of the reasons I befriended him. All our classmates had nodded in agreement when Mr. Dunning, the physics master, hit him over the head with a physics book and said, 'You'll never get anywhere, Chrystal!' We were all wrong, because

IBM saw something in him, and John rose high in that massive company. Either their corporate ethics, or living in the USA, or even that hit over the head changed him for the better.

The contact lenses that replaced the thick glasses of Maidstone Grammar School were special, sparkling in a certain light like a macho Mary Poppins. Whatever it was, John was now truly impressive, and it all made my officer training in the RAF seem pretty inadequate. Nevertheless, he and Elisabeth couldn't have been more welcoming and their wedding and the reception at a country club afterwards was perfect in all ways. Five days in Connecticut re-kindled my spirits and I was grateful to them both. When John invited me back to ski in Vermont at Christmastime I was sorely tempted, because I knew that this Christmas by myself was going to be difficult.

With my batteries recharged things were at last looking up and I put my new impetus in to finding a house. I centred my search around West Chiltington in West Sussex because it was convenient for Gatwick and Bill Brennen and his family lived there. A fourteenth century church, golf course and four very nice pubs all added to the charm.

I'd looked there briefly once before; when we had all come down from Scotland to see the Steyning house we had quickly rejected a house in the village called Briarwood. It was still for sale so I looked again. The owners were now as desperate to sell as I was to move, so without much haggling my offer was accepted. I talked about moving in at the beginning of 1982, and that had a nice feel to it; a new year, a new house and a new beginning.

But first was Christmas, which this year was going to be like no other and it scared me. The last ten with the children had been wonderful, and the last seven in Scotland especially so, made almost magical by our three young children and the prospect of almost guaranteed snow between Christmas and New Year.

We always made a big thing of Christmas, with a day set aside in Glasgow for the two of us to buy the presents, but then we looked at our three children with such pride that, inevitably, Adrienne and I would scurry into Helensburgh to buy them some more. Christmas Eve meant the family carol service at St Andrew's Church, and it wasn't until we were certain that they were all fast asleep that I delivered, in my Father Christmas outfit, those presents to the foot of their beds.

After opening presents on Christmas Day of 1980 we had driven down to Iris's house in Sheffield for our Christmas dinner, coming back to Helensburgh in time for the thick snow of New Year. The Gare Loch was particularly chilly when I jumped off the pier on New Year's morning with Nigel and his friend Mark for the annual charity jump. Christmas 1980 holiday was full of sledging and ice skating and fun, rounded off nicely with the Kelvin Hall Circus in Glasgow.

Christmas 1981 would be so very different. People asked, 'What are you doing for Christmas?' with a sort of worried look, which only added to the tension. I didn't know what to do. Volunteers were always needed to fly over Christmas, but I wasn't sure just how emotional I would be and I couldn't take a chance with flying. I was invited to spend the holiday with Colin's family, but they deserved some freedom from sadness at that special time. I thought about my parents, and I knew I'd be made as welcome as we all had been for the memorable Christmas of 1979; one of my favourite photos is of Anna-Jane walking hand in hand with my father, wearing her new nurse's outfit on Christmas morning.

But my parents were still in shock, and I didn't want more of my sadness spilling over them. Eventually I decided on something very different; I would take up John Chrystal's invitation and learn to ski in Vermont. Definitely different enough to divert my mind from Christmases past.

On Thursday 17 December, as I'd done just weeks before, I caught the Skytrain to New York, and John drove me to his timbered house in Connecticut. We left early next morning, so by the middle of the afternoon John, his wife Elisabeth and I were all on the bitterly cold ski slopes of Vermont. They had their own skis, so they shot off to black runs, while I hired all my equipment and signed up for basic lessons. I thought it would help to have a bright purple ski suit!

Over the next four days I found out that even with a bright purple ski suit, skiing wasn't easy. It was, however, the perfect mental diversion and I decided that spending the holiday in the USA was a good idea. It definitely was, until we all returned to Connecticut three days before Christmas. Knowing that John and Elisabeth would spend Christmas in New York with Elisabeth's mother, I'd gratefully accepted a kind invitation from John's friend Anne Smith to spend the few days of Christmas at her home in Cos Cob. Anne was one of John's serial fiancées, and a hyperactive lady who I had already met and liked, and seemingly bore no grudge about John dumping her to marry Elisabeth.

Cos Cob is a quaint and lovely New England village, and she showed me the old village fire engine, all polished ready for action next door, and the big decorated Christmas tree in the centre of the village around which we would sing carols on Christmas Eve. Like the set of an Andy Williams Christmas show it was all perfect, colourful and lovely.

Anne worked tirelessly to make me comfortable in her lovely house, until she went off to work on that first day. I was surrounded by the spirit of Christmas; a Christmas tree and scores of beautiful cards and Christmas decorations inside the house, and more schmaltzy 'glitterings' outside. I turned on the radio, and heard Barry Manilow singing 'Weekend in New England' so many times that I got to hate it. Perhaps because every word described where I was or how I felt.

At any other Christmas I would have loved every sight and every sound. But not this one, and I'm ashamed to say, it all got too much for me, and I booked the Christmas Eve flight back home. I feel awful still about rejecting Anne's wonderful generosity and guilty about not coping with it. But at that moment I needed to be closer to home, wherever that was, and certainly nearer my photos and memories. By the time I disembarked at Gatwick Christmas was almost over, and although I wasn't proud of what I had done it was one way of making Christmas disappear.

Anne deserves great credit for understanding and forgiving me. She came to visit me in England a few weeks later, and I met up with her in the mid-eighties near Mougins, in the south of France, where she was working for IBM. For some reason however she never invited me to Christmas in Cos Cob again.

13

Christmas was a huge emotional milestone, and with its passing the pressure was lifted. My brother Colin, his wife Jill and his two young children had shared their small house with me for nine months, and without them, and their help at the most difficult of times, I'm not certain I could have coped with life, let alone return to work. Now it was time to move on. It was only me that left the house, Sophie my dog stayed and was now a much-loved member of their family.

My new house was a bit of a mess, which was probably the reason it hadn't sold for over a year. I looked forward to working on it, but the best thing for me was seeing my belongings again, delivered after almost a year in storage. Now I had space and my own telephone, and for the next few winter months, less flying. Things had to happen in Miami.

The anniversary of the accident was coming up, and I still hadn't heard anything from the Miami police, or indeed anybody, and Alistair was apparently still busy.

I tried phoning Miami again, searching for somebody who knew anything about my case and a possible prosecution. I established that the Dade County Police covered the area of the accident, and eventually got through to them. It seemed as though they had accidents like mine every week, because it didn't ring a particular bell. 'We will look into it, please call us back in a week'.

A week later I was told that the accident was still being

looked in to. I was feeling stronger now, time was passing and that response wasn't good enough. We would have to go to Miami very soon. This was not how things were supposed to happen. What could I do that I hadn't already done?

The anniversary came up, and of course I spent that day in Sheffield, which made me even more aware that my family deserved answers. Sleeping became difficult again and people said, for the only time in my life, that I had lost too much weight.

Rather than pace up and down the room, I'd taken to jogging around the roads of West Chiltington. In an attempt to put things into boxes and clear my mind, I turned to music, my music, and for a while it became crucial, linking me to 'those times' and those four people. It didn't matter to me if it was corny or morbid (which it wasn't) or wistful (which it probably was), but those pieces meant something and unbottled thoughts and emotions locked inside me.

I used to sing, 'When a child is born' loudly in Nigel's bedroom at Christmastime, with the girls joining in. I had sung (and danced to), 'By the time I get to Phoenix', with the girls after the good news of the house being sold. The truly wistful songs of Bread just seemed to sum up how I felt, and, I believe, transferred some of the sadness from me. Now, in my own house, I could play those songs and others as loudly and as often as I liked. The best answer to my problems was to return to Miami, but still my legal advisor was unperturbed and would come 'when he could'. Though I knew he wasn't interested in a prosecution, I was calmed somewhat by Alistair's confidence that justice would take its course; it was the USA after all.

I needed some light relief, and that came with a phone call

from Jackie Bishop. I had only met her briefly, at a barbeque Adrienne had organised to welcome a visiting teacher of students with learning disabilities from San Francisco. A schoolmate of our friend Alison Risk, Jackie was at our barbeque because she knew Alison and loved parties. Her call said she was just back from Hong Kong where she had been briefly married and then divorced. She was about to start a new job at Gatwick and needed a place to live for two or three months until she found somewhere more permanent.

Jackie was a fast mover. She moved in two days later and stayed for over a year. Always lively, always ready for a party, her presence in those early days stopped me from becoming too morose, surrounded as I now was by the family memorabilia. I hadn't even noticed, until she bravely pointed it out, that the interior of Briarwood was becoming a replica of our house in Scotland, even to the extent of sourcing the same Werner 'peacock' curtains to go with the same wall lights. With dozens of photos and big pictures of the family around every room, Jackie ventured that the house looked like a mausoleum. I was shocked, but I looked around and saw that she was right. I did keep the curtains, but I restricted the family photos to one room, with just a few more on the piano and in my bedroom.

Bill Brennan lived less than a mile away, and I was quickly brought into his wide social circle in the village, which included the local dramatic society. He took the lead in *My Fair Lady* and was described by a neighbour as, 'Better than Rex Harrison', while I helped screw seats onto the raised auditorium. He was a success, but I was a failure, because I dropped a vital script between the boards that I'd spent two hours connecting, and the whole section of seating had to be disassembled.

Quite often, in fine weather, my parents drove down to see me, and my mother liked lunch at the thatched Oddfellows Arms in Pulborough, followed by a small 'sweetheart stout'. My parents were deeply scarred by the accident, my mother especially. She hugged me tightly at the end of every visit, something she had never done before Adrienne came on to the scene, but now it was more heartfelt and intense. There was sadness in their eyes, as probably there was in mine. The loss of Adrienne and the children on top of a difficult life raising six children with little money and an often-overbearing husband seemed to have finally worn her down. Money was always tight, though my father worked hard in his summer holidays by picking hops, apples and pears in the Kentish fields to supplement his wage as a lorry driver, then bus driver, and latterly a bus inspector. As children our only holidays were two-day outings on a brown Maidstone Corporation double-decker bus, to the Kent coast, usually to Margate or Ramsgate, and our journey was free if my father drove the bus!

My parents looked old now. Adrienne's warm outgoing nature and the loveliness of our children had etched something into the hearts of both of them which I doubt they had seen before, and that's why the loss had hit them so hard. I always looked forward to seeing them in my new house and they enjoyed the drive down from Maidstone.

It was good to have Jackie in the house, not least because she liked to conjure up a party. Her boyfriend, Stephen, lived in Cape Town (she didn't lead a simple life) and she asked if Stephen's brother and sister-in-law from Cape Town could stay for a weekend. That was how I met Anne and Barry from Constantia, Cape Town, and so began a lifelong friendship with them, and with Cape Town.

Jackie's social manifesto got bigger and bigger, and she persuaded me to have a summer barbeque on the day of the village 6km fun run. It became a yearly event, and nobody seemed to mind that food followed by a run was not perhaps the best way of doing things. I was in a lovely sociable village and was getting sucked into Jackie's social whirl which generally kept my spirits high.

Things were looking up, until an early morning phone call told me I that my mother had died suddenly from a heart attack. She had seemed well when I'd seen her just a few days before and hadn't been ill. I was totally shocked, and I fell against the patio window. It was some minutes and after a cup of tea from Jackie before I felt able to phone my father and say I would drive down to his house.

The rest of my family were there and already discussing the funeral. I was the second youngest but now considered the expert on funerals, so managed to slow things down and talk about my mother in life rather than death. I stayed with my father for a few days and gave the undertaker an arbitrary date for the funeral, to be held at St Margaret's Church, Barming in Kent.

Just before the service, we learned that my brother Derek would not be coming, apparently thinking that the date had been chosen deliberately knowing his daughter couldn't attend.

Suspicions and conspiracy theories always abounded in my family, even on days like that, and I left that funeral secretly glad that I'd moved away from it all twenty years before. (At Colin's funeral at the same church some years later, half my family sat on one side of the church not really speaking to the other half on the other side. I sat in the middle, in all ways.)

The service was short, and as I walked out of the attractive little church, I saw Iris from Sheffield and Adrienne's sister, Pat. It was a surprise, and very welcome after such a sad day. It meant to me that I was still 'one of their family' and it was just what I needed.

A difficult day suddenly seemed brighter. I returned home the next day, buoyed by their efforts and with new resolve to get things moving in Miami. No police investigation after twenty months was ridiculous, and surely there couldn't be an investigation without asking me, the main witness, 'What actually happened?' Just as I would ask them, 'What was the can of drink I saw in the driver's hand?'

I had to go to Miami, with or without Alistair.

Another busy summer flying season had finished, so I could get away more or less anytime. Having had no contact from anybody, exactly where to go in Miami and who to see was more of a problem. I plumped for the district attorney for Dade County. I found a telephone number and I made an appointment, and now, at long last, I was definitely going.

My plan created waves in the Sheffield family, crumbling the image of Iris's son being my legal saviour, and she was in tears when she phoned me. But I could wait no longer. Surely they could see that, and it saddened me that I was the only one who was champing at the bit; didn't they want to see justice done? It wasn't long before Alistair phoned, with new energy and an apology. Though he was 'up to his eyes' in very important things which couldn't be left, he was *definitely* on the case and would work out a date. It would be before Christmas.

Forever restless since the accident, and now facing more

trauma in Miami, I needed to escape. I thought back to a letter sent to me from Jim and Trudie Concoran, who lived in California. In 1979 Scotland was right at the forefront of teaching people with learning disabilities and in June of that year Trudie was seconded for a month from San Francisco to Jordanhill College in Glasgow.

Adrienne invited her and her husband over to Helensburgh for a barbeque to meet our neighbours and friends. After a very enjoyable evening Trudie had made the first entry in our new visitor's book. 'What a perfectly elegant evening, and how we deeply appreciate your thoughtfulness… we will be taking away such fond memories of Helensburgh'. We had met briefly at appropriately, the Caledonian Club in San Francisco on our short family holiday to Disneyland in 1980. I now thought back to their very warm letter after the accident, inviting me to stay with them in Los Gatos. If they'd still have me, now was the time to go.

Los Gatos is in the foothills of the Santa Cruz mountains, just south of San Jose, and it is as lovely as it sounds. Their house overlooked the valley, and in fact it was two houses, and for a week I occupied one of them, with my own swimming pool. It was just what I needed, and I came back from California having much nicer thoughts about the USA, but wondering if the upcoming visit to the Dade County district attorney might change all that.

I was newly energised after the week away, and had the upper hand with Alistair, now desperate to restore his image with his mother as my helper. For a while at least, he was proactive. He couldn't make his promised 'before Christmas', but he had arranged time off for the first week in January 1983.

The drip-drip of hungry American lawyers wanting to take up a civil case was now just a drip, and according to Alistair's 'gleanings', from what they had to say, the fall-off in interest was because Mr. Anderson, the driver who caused my family's deaths, had no assets. He had only the state minimum third-party insurance cover of $20,000, which made him 'legal', but those lawyers had established that he was unemployed, and without resources. Certainly, they said, Mr. Anderson himself was not viable for a hefty civil claim, but *there might be other avenues.*

At last I had a visit to Miami to look forward to, although the name of the city itself sent shivers down my back. Much like my visits to the grave, I wanted to be there, but I didn't.

Coming up first was Christmas and not wanting the problems of the previous one, I chose the simple solution of volunteering to work. On Christmas Eve I flew to Faro in Portugal, spending three days with the crew in a hotel there before flying back. All six crew were 'escapees', running away from Christmas for one reason or another. A psychiatrist would have had a field day.

Everybody tried hard, but most of us were looking at our watches, willing it to be over and another year ticked off. Finally it was, and for me, time to go back to Miami with my unpaid legal advisor.

14

Alistair and I met at Heathrow for the daylight flight to Miami. British Airways had generously given us club class tickets, which allowed us to talk with some degree of privacy as well as cushioning my inbuilt fears of going back to that awful place. I'd already arranged an appointment with the Dade County district attorney and booked us both into a hotel near where we would meet our prospective lawyers.

When I mentioned the district attorney, it brought no response from Alistair. I was beginning to question whether, away from the gaze of his Sheffield family, he was interested at all.

He insisted he was, so perhaps I was lucky to have sitting beside me a legal advisor and close relation all wrapped into one, albeit that he was only interested in a possible civil claim. For that I would need an American lawyer and Alistair would help me find one.

It was almost two years since the accident, but the delay didn't seem to bother him as much as it did me. I put that down to the imperturbability of a wise lawyer, and not the negligence of somebody who wasn't really bothered.

I was back in the city that gave me nightmares, yet I was pleased to be there. After checking us into our hotel in downtown Miami I went straight to bed, partly because of the long flight, but more to do with being back in that part of the world.

Early morning on a workday in any American city is

invigorating. I was among work-driven, shirt-sleeved business-men, fuelled by coffee and seemingly with places to go and people to see. Today I had to make things happen.

Over breakfast we reviewed the day's plan, starting with my imminent visit to the district attorney. My expectations of a stiff but appropriate sentence for Anderson raised Alistair's hackles and he mounted his hobby horse, a horse that he was still riding forty years later. He believed that only the crime is relevant to a prosecution, not the consequences. In other words, the law should pay no regard to the fact that four people were killed and should treat Anderson as if he had merely scratched the bumper of our car.

Highly theoretical, I thought, wondering out loud if attempted murder got the same sentence as murder. But now was neither the time nor place to argue. Leaving Alistair sitting in the hotel contacting prospective lawyers, I set off to see the man in charge of public prosecutions in Dade County Miami. I couldn't wait. I'd find out why I'd heard nothing from them in two years, even wondering if perhaps I was to blame for the accident, and they were trying to protect me. This meeting was crucial.

The district attorney welcomed me with an outstretched hand and was polite but, I thought, sheepish from the outset, which made me think that something was being held back.

He handed me a copy of the two-page accident report, the first time that I'd seen it. It was just a very brief outline of the accident, compiled by Trooper Haveard, presumably the first policeman on the scene, though there was also the name of another trooper, as the assigned investigator.

One thing leapt out from the page. I read that my son Nigel

was taken separately to the American Hospital in Miami, where they had tried to revive him. Those words shook me then and they shake me now.

The sparse report said that our car had cartwheeled and glanced off trees before going into the water, which was around twenty-five feet deep.

I saw *Under arrest; Robert Anderson* followed by *Improper turn.* Then I read *Anderson came from the northern edge of the road (SR-90) into the Eastbound traffic lane.*

The report didn't mention that he was in reverse without lights and had a can of drink in his hand.

I saw the names of four witnesses, who presumably were in the bus that followed me. According to the district attorney, the witnesses confirmed that I was not to blame, and the visibility was so good that our headlights would have been seen from half a mile. It wasn't till later that I wondered how the DA knew that; did he interview the witnesses, or was there a further report? Inspector Matt Butler, head of the Serious Collision Team for Dorset, Devon and Cornwall, was to tell me much later that the report I saw, including as it did a file reference number, and the mention of witnesses and photographs, indicated that a much more comprehensive accident file must have existed. According to Inspector Butler I should have known what was in that accident file and asked to comment on it as the principal witness.

My first question, and one that I'd been waiting to ask for two years, got a direct reply: 'The accident report has been compiled and Mr. Anderson will be prosecuted'. I assumed he was talking about the flimsy report before me.

Asking, 'When where and how?' drew a shrug of the

Taking Nigel aged ten to Orkney and Shetland from Glasgow in a Vickers
Viscount Spring 1980

That same summer on the beach at Fréjus

August 1980. Adrienne, the twins, and Nigel outside a restaurant in St Raph.

Me with the family just before buying a painting on the quay in St Tropez

Anna-Jane and Lucy-Claire, sound asleep and secure

Just a few years later, ready for action outside our old white front door

May 1980. With Nigel's friend Mark, at the summit of Ben Lomond

Adrienne and Nigel, always happy together. In Glen Fruin, where we walked most Sunday mornings

The girls outside our newly painted green front door

(right) Sledging down the Rest and be Thankful. Unusually Anna-Jane looking the more confident

Beside the pool at Le Pin de la Lègue caravan site

The girls and their ten-year-old big brother

Firlands our house in Helensburgh, with a For Sale sign outside
I wish it hadn't sold - September 1980

About to leave the Holiday Inn Sarasota Florida - February 1981
Our last photo together, taken by Nigel
Both photos were damaged by Everglades water

My last Boeing 747 take-off from Heathrow heading for Boston

My last Concorde take-off from Heathrow, flying to New York

About to take-off from Wombleton for Scarborough in my shiny Streak
adow, 'C'est si bon'. At a fraction of the cost, and far quicker to get airborne
than either of the above, but not bought by British Airways!

My loved and loving family, as we were and as we were meant to be

shoulders and a repeat of the promise, as did my question about me giving testimony as the main witness. As did, 'What was in the can of drink? Was his alcohol level checked? What about the lack of lights?'

The only real answer was a repeated 'Mr. Anderson will be prosecuted,' and the DA couldn't say where or when. He changed tack with a very basic question which astonished me: 'Tell me what happened that night.'

It was almost two years after the accident, two years in which I'd been a phone call and a letter away, and two years after I should have been asked that very question. But I wondered, had I somehow pricked his conscience, was he going to take a personal interest and get things moving?

Then, out of the blue, he said that Anderson was truly sorry. I assumed he would be, but just the way he said that, and his previous question, 'What happened?' made me wonder if he had told me the truth, and that a prosecution of Mr. Anderson had long ago been swept under the carpet, finished, and forgotten. Did he say Anderson was sorry as a sop, a substitute for an adequate prosecution? My last question, 'When will the court case be scheduled?' just got a wave of the hand.

I left his office disillusioned and confused. All I could hang on to were his words, 'Mr. Anderson will be prosecuted.' He didn't convince me of anything, other than wanting me out of his hair and back in the UK. Alistair's presence would have helped, as a lawyer and as a witness to what was said, but he was half a mile away. I saw in him what I'd just seen in the district attorney, and I began to wonder which came first, the coldness or the legal profession.

I was convinced throughout our meeting that there was no

impetus for a prosecution. My family had died, I was not to blame, and yet as far as information went, I was out there on the periphery. Something odd was happening. Was it because I was white and living in the UK, well away from the scene of the accident and the home of Mr. Anderson, who was black?

Race was definitely a very sensitive subject in Miami at that time; just recently serious rioting had led to the deaths of at least eighteen people and $100 million worth of damage in that same Dade County. When the DA talked to me about Mr. Anderson saying sorry, he had touched upon the problems of the area. Miami authorities had every reason to take a pragmatic line instead of sorting justice; racists would have had a field day if the matter of a black man being responsible for the deaths of four white people had become high profile. To quietly sweep everything under the carpet and take advantage of me living on the other side of the ocean must at least have been a temptation.

I met up with Alistair back at the hotel where he was looking through the briefs that he had brought with him from London, all rolled and neatly wrapped in coloured ribbon. I thought back an hour, and what I had just been through. He was a busy man, but he'd grown up with Adrienne and was godfather to Nigel, and he'd preferred to sit there rather than accompany me to my meeting with the district attorney. But it was a highly emotional time, and perhaps he had his reasons.

He *was* interested in the civil case, and we began to talk about the car insurance situation in the USA which, we had discovered, was very different from the rest of the world. The lawyers had put much emphasis on Anderson's 'State Minimum $20,000' third-party insurance, so now we needed to find out why. The US was obviously a foreign country in all ways, but I took comfort in knowing that I'd ticked the boxes on the car hire form and been assured by the agent that I was 'fully covered'. Could anybody have done any more?

We set off to find a lawyer, and met several, with me, the layman surrounded by legal eagles, Alistair included. First came a bombshell: In Florida, there was something called a 'statute of limitations' for wrongful death, which meant any civil case had to start by the 17 February, just five weeks away. I looked at Alistair, surprised that he had not been aware of such a basic deadline when he had kept delaying our visit throughout 1981 and 1982. Now everything was a rush.

Then another shock. Despite ticking all the boxes on the car rental form, and those reassuring words from the agent, I had set off unknowingly in that hired car with just that State Minimum Insurance. Nothing else was on offer, which was absurd in the country where you are most likely to be sued for vast sums of money. It was for just that reason I had asked, 'Am I fully insured?' yet I had driven away with the same minimum insurance as Anderson, with nothing else offered to me.

It was no consolation to be told that the rental agent must have assumed I was American, despite my accent, my address on the form and the fact that I had arrived at an international airport. An American renter would have been covered by the insurance on his own car at home, whereas a European's car insurance only stayed with his car in the garage. That we could see, was the big difference between the USA and other countries, creating a loophole that I had fallen into along with thousands of other non-American renters. All this in a state where one in four drivers was completely uninsured. (This was something that Alistair and I later highlighted on Breakfast TV which took even the chairman of the Association of British Travel Agents (ABTA) by surprise.)

As time went on during our interviews with lawyers, I could see we were going around in circles. Perhaps my heightened sensitivity sharpened my antennae, but it seemed that ten words were being used when one would do, and everyone except me was either speaking or nodding appreciatively. Eventually I had to say that our case should be simple: when I rented that car, I should have been offered the same insurance that protected American drivers. 'Oh yes,' they said. The fog cleared, and it was agreed that our claim would be that I was neither offered that essential insurance nor told that I didn't have it.

Our last interview of the day brought two lawyers who were quite different from those who had gone before. Richard B was tall and smartly dressed and looked every inch the part. His colleague Carl S was small, bald, untidy, and hunched up, looking every centimetre like one of the Marx Brothers. The straight man did the talking; the other wandered round the room like a hungry lion, scratching his bald head and even sitting briefly in the corner. I scratched my head too, rubbed my eyes and wondered if the scene was real.

Incredibly, Alistair was impressed, and after what I thought was Act One of a play, he said I should employ them. No matter that there were two to pay, rather than one, or that they wanted fifty per cent of any compensation. Or that they asked for 'stage payments', whereas most of the others worked on a no-win, no-fee basis.

Alistair, as a high-flying lawyer in London knew what he was talking about. So, against my own instincts, I employed them.

I had no choice now we had such a tight deadline.

We got down to more detail. The 'thinker', Carl S, came up with the master plan, an embroidered version of my simple thoughts. According to him, there was absolutely no doubt we would win, and that the compensation would be several million dollars. In that case, I wondered to Alistair, why do they want their stage payments? Alistair said it cemented their commitment. (Letters that surfaced later show that lawyer B was the front man who had very little to do with my case after the initial meeting. Lawyer S made all the moves, and there are several indications that he was never sure of his ground, often asking for help.)

We were told there was no time to lose. Though the legal system ran slowly, that didn't matter as long as the case was set in motion by 17 February. Apparently, there was only one biggish hurdle to get over, and that was to persuade a district judge that there was a case to answer. If he decided there was, (our new lawyers were ecstatically confident), the case would then go before a jury at a county court and, according to our double-act, winning there was almost a formality. Easy. The jury, they said, were bound to be sympathetic, so we would win. The compensation would be at least $5 million, and even allowing for the 50% to my lawyers, there would be enough to create something really worthwhile in memory of my family. I'd already thought of a bursary or foundation and made it absolutely plain that every dollar of any money I received would be used for that.

Alistair and I returned to London, leaving our lawyers to their work and with me pinning my hopes on the words, 'Mr. Anderson will be prosecuted' words from the district attorney.

The USA surely knew right from wrong.

With the newly started civil case, I believed there wasn't even a whiff of uncertainty, and I thought of the square-jawed lawyers with gravelly voices I saw in TV courtroom dramas; they always won on the side of right. Our chosen two lawyers didn't look or sound or even seem like that, but I had a legal advisor who was more than capable of dotting all the i's and crossing all the t's. However, with the tight deadline of the statute of limitations, he hadn't got off to the best of starts.

*

On 16 February 1983, one day before the deadline, my new legal duo in Miami duly submitted four lawsuits, one for each death. This was perhaps their first and pretty basic mistake, because the 'offence' they were citing was committed when the car was hired, which was five days earlier. There were two defendants, Dollar Rent A Car at Miami Airport and National Union, their public liability insurers.

The lawsuits were issued on three counts: negligence, breach of contract and misrepresentation. The hub of our case was that I had not been offered the level of insurance that an American renter would have automatically had, and that only with *that* insurance would I have been adequately covered. Dollar should have made it their business to know that at an international airport there was a fair chance that the renter would be from outside of the USA, and would need UM (uninsured motorist) insurance.

My lawyers asked for an initial $1500, followed by stage payments and then 50% of any award. With the lawsuits issued my civil case was on its way. Alistair was happy, and back to his work. I'd bowed to the legal experts, with misgivings about the abilities of our chosen lawyers and the commitment of Alistair. Even in Miami, he spent so much time with his rolled-up briefs from London that I asked if his mind was there. Not for the first time I offered to pay him, to get that full commitment. Not for the first time he said my case had his full focus, he trusted the two lawyers, and we should let them get on with their work.

Time would tell, but already I had no confidence in those two lawyers, and I checked everything, starting with the lawsuits. The defendant was the small Dollar outlet at Miami Airport, and in a potentially multi-million claim, that didn't seem right. I spoke to the British Franchise Association, and their advice was to always include the top of a franchise pyramid, in this case, the mammoth Dollar Rent A Car in California. They quoted a similar case in New York, O'Boyle v Avis Rent a Car, where the parent company (Avis) was brought into the lawsuit. I passed their advice to Alistair, who dismissed it saying, 'They know what they are doing'. But my conversations later raised doubts and it was possibly a very big mistake

Despite getting legal advice here from Alistair and paying for it in the USA, I already had bad vibes about everything. I waited to hear from the district attorney but expected to hear nothing. I didn't know what else I could do; because my voice wasn't being heard and the whole subject was depressing. I just knew the civil case would fail, though my advisor said it wouldn't. I could sack them all and start again, but the statute of limitations deadline had passed, and presumably any new lawyer would have to use those same wrongly issued lawsuits. For the time being at least, I would have to stick with Alistair and just hope he was right, both in his choice of lawyers and the path they were taking. At least that would keep relations on an even keel with Alistair's disciples in Sheffield, especially Iris, his mother. In my taut emotional state that was perhaps the most important thing to me.

I needed to do something, if only to rid me of the gnawing feeling that I had let my family down. I arranged a meeting with Richard Luce, the MP for the area I had just moved into. He promised to pass on my concerns to the Foreign Office, just as John Stanley MP had done eighteen months earlier. The reply then had only counselled patience, something that was now exhausted and I could only hope that another prod from an MP following my visit to the district attorney might get a more specific response.

No such luck. The reply, a couple of weeks later was on very official paper from the Foreign Office and ostensibly from (it was signed by) Malcolm Rifkind. As before, it was disappointingly bland, full of meaningless platitudes that were so easy to write but so difficult to read. It got me nowhere, other than thinking that nobody in authority, either in Miami or London, really cared.

Suddenly Alistair became hyperactive, or at least compared to what I had seen before. He prepared a lengthy and carefully scripted press release to 'get out there' the dangerous insurance situation for European drivers renting a car in Florida. Trusting it was all for the right reasons and not to enhance his legal profile, I went along with it, although I had resisted publicity after the accident because I didn't want to be part of anything involving my family that might appear ghoulish in any way. He sent the press release to breakfast TV in the UK and to our lawyers, hoping that it might help them appreciate the crucial difference in car insurance between their country and ours. TV-am responded quickly and a date was set for a recorded session at my house in West Chiltington.

Lynn Faulds Wood drove down from London to interview us. Alistair put across very clearly the insurance loophole we had exposed. In contrast, the Chief Executive of ABTA, interviewed in his office, looked very uncomfortable, showing complete ignorance about the whole matter. It was a lot of 'Haven't we done that?', followed by lots of, 'Yes, of course, we'll do that', all making the viewer wonder if he was even going to close the stable door after the horse had bolted. Lynn asked me if she could borrow the six hours of recent video I had taken of the family, so they could use clips edited from it. I hesitated, but Lynn's integrity shone through, and I gave her the videos.

On the morning of the TV broadcast, I was nervous about how the clips would be shown. But I needn't have worried because it was all done brilliantly, with a closing beautiful but emotive shot of Lucy playing the piano. I was pleased to keep in touch with Lynn Faulds Wood and years later she went to great lengths to find me a recording of that TV interview with those precious clips of my family.

The TV-am broadcast brought a big response from others who had fallen foul of car insurance in the USA, Florida especially. Further tales of sadness I just couldn't face at that time, but I did send them off to the lawyers in Miami.

The summer of 1983 brought the most intense flying of my career so far, with nearly ninety flying hours in July (a total not passed until I began crossing the Atlantic on the Boeing

767 and 747).

Between flights I squeezed in drives to Sheffield for family birthdays whenever possible, always pleased to stay at Iris's house overnight. I began my routine of keeping a torch in the car so I could maintain my lifelong habit of making the graveside my first port of call in Sheffield. But the intensity of flying that summer meant that Miami needed to go in to the background.

In any case, my quest for a prosecution had come to a dead stop; there was nothing more I could do other than wait to hear from Miami. I was happier (though not happy) to let the civil case bubble on, through 1983 and then in to 1984. I had to pin my hopes on Alistair, trusting that as godfather to Nigel and virtually a brother to Adrienne, he would surely be doing his level best; and all might not be lost.

Half way through the year my lodger Jackie finally moved out to get married to David, her third husband and umpteenth boyfriend. She had stayed in my house for over a year, having said that it would be for three months, but now she had found a house *and* a husband. I'd enjoyed having her in the house, and would miss her social whirl. Though very attractive, we never had a relationship (her idea not mine) and I enjoyed her selection of boyfriends almost as much as she did. One was a sailor, and not long after she'd said *hello* to him, I was enjoying summer evenings sailing from Brighton Marina on his big yacht. I was especially disappointed when he got the heave-ho from Jackie, because he was my favourite.

Now she was moving on, but I continued her idea of having a yearly barbeque before the village fun run. The numbers coming to the event and the barbeque got bigger and bigger every year, and the run more competitive. Some of the men even trained for it and ate sparingly from the barbeque before-hand. Controversy crept in, and some competitors who finished way ahead of me in the race couldn't understand how I was awarded a silver cup. I had to explain that my particular prize was awarded for artistic impression, rather than speed. And the sole judge of that was my friend Bill Brennen, who presented the cup that still sits in my house. More difficult to explain, especially to those who had trained hard, was the wrong start time I gave to some of the runners one year, which meant they arrived at the starting line fifteen minutes after the rest had left.

15

I wanted an end to everything to do with Miami, and a clear outcome to the battles I'd fought for three long years. I've never liked the word 'closure' but that was exactly what I wanted. My thoughts on my family would never close, but to hear something, anything from the Miami police would mean that somebody 'over there' actually noticed that four innocent people had been killed.

It didn't seem much to ask for, but sometimes I thought the lack of action was driving me mad. I trod a fine line, keeping my concentration when I had to work without letting it slip, even for a second, because of what was happening, or not happening, in Miami. I had dual goals, both so important to me. Not to let my family slip away in silence, and not to lose my job. A poor third was winning the civil case that I'd just embarked on, but my family seemed poles apart from the values I'd already observed in the murky world of money-obsessed American lawyers. But I had to stick with it; if all else failed a successful outcome would at least lay down some sort of indelible marker concerning what happened on 17 February 1981. I wouldn't be holding my breath.

*

All I had to show for my efforts was a promise from the district attorney, two bland assurances from the Foreign Office and a shaky last-minute start from the two lawyers in Miami. Worst of all, nobody really seemed bothered. No one picks sadness given a choice, and my hyperactive demeanour, playing squash and tennis, jogging around the village and doing big jobs around the house was something that neighbours, colleagues, people in Scotland and family in Maidstone were keen to latch on to as a sign that everything was behind me. In truth it was a diversion, to keep my restless mind in check. Just the name Miami gave me nightmares and seemed to push any hope for a more stable life further and further away. Friends everywhere were getting on with their lives, and who could blame them? But thankfully stalwarts remained, most especially my brother Colin, Bill Brennen who was now just down the road and always ready with advice, and Gail and Ian Standing from Helensburgh, who persevered with sometimes one-way conversations and kept me in their much appreciated family loop. Support was mostly beyond the remit of my own family except for Colin, but my sister's husband David suddenly became a lifeline, and phoned just about every day. I needed that input.

I think my job kept me sane, though I suppose the passengers would have hoped that my sanity kept my job. Flying to me was the perfect panacea. Nothing about work was ever the same, I flew at different times, to different places, and with different people, and perhaps being above the world and looking down had its psychological benefits. Concentrating on the job in hand kept my brain ticking over and forced the accident into the background, and of course there was no leeway given in the intense, routine simulator and route checks, (flying a normal route with passengers, but with someone sitting alongside or behind checking you), that I had to pass. My stability now was my job, so I needed to knuckle down and carve out another fifteen years with British Airways. I often wondered, when I stood still for a moment at home, if there would be a downside to my hanging on by a thread existence while pretending all was well.

Counselling wasn't a big thing then, but British Airways had offered it just after the accident, and I'd turned it down. Now, the few people who saw through my veneer suggested it might help. I gave it lots of thought, before deciding not to disturb a hornet's nest and perhaps put in jeopardy the one thing that kept me going, my job. I carried on being hyperactive and I found peace in playing my music and sorting through photographs. I had six hours of video tape of my family, but it would be a long time before I was stable enough to watch them. That would certainly disturb another hornet's nest.

I'd started what became my lifelong routine of driving up to the churchyard in Sheffield at least five times a year, on each birthday and our wedding anniversary, and it was something I looked forward to for weeks beforehand.

Sussex to Sheffield is an awkward journey, and sometimes because of the busy summer work schedules I had to drive up and back in a day. Generally though, I stayed at Iris's house, and in return I would do jobs around the house, rewarded on a Sunday with a perfect Sunday lunch complete with authentic Yorkshire puddings, all served from her hostess trolley. The jobs often involved repairing the fence between her house and the pub next door which kept falling down due to either my poor workmanship or the surplus of Yorkshire ale in the pub's customers. At Iris's house I felt close to Adrienne and the children, and our togetherness in history and sorrow made it difficult to criticise her son, even though I continued to doubt his input as my legal advisor.

The future of Peter, Adrienne's younger brother who had Downs Syndrome was yet another legacy of the accident. She grew up beside him, producing a special and unique bond that was lovely to see. Peter's face always shone with happiness and everybody loved him, but it was to Adrienne that he always looked.

Iris in many ways had been a lifelong guardian for Adrienne, supporting Adrienne's mother after the early death of her father. Now, quite wonderfully, Iris wanted to be a guardian for Peter, partly I think because of her love for Adrienne. If my visits to Sheffield were on a Sunday I would collect Peter for Iris's excellent lunch, during which one of us would say how happy Adrienne would be to see the three of us sitting there together. If I was in Sheffield on a Saturday, Peter and I would watch the football at Bramall Lane or Hillsborough.

Ecclesall churchyard was massive, and on my first visits it had all looked surprisingly neat. Three years later grass, weeds and even small trees were growing unchecked, and the now familiar old headstones beside the path leaned drunkenly, almost submerged under a tide of advancing greenery. The churchyard had become very personal to me, so I arranged to see the vicar.

Over a cup of tea in the vicarage, he confirmed a recent change of policy. A church committee had decided that the whole area should become a natural wilderness. Apparently the area was so big, and many of the graves so old that it was economically impossible to keep things neat and tidy; not the sort of thing I wanted to hear, so soon after I had chosen his churchyard for a literally lifelong-and-beyond relationship. I thought of the small, picturesque location of my mother's funeral two years before; perhaps after all I should have chosen the Barming churchyard. I was disappointed but my mind didn't work quickly enough to say that cleanliness was next to godliness. I did ask if I could arrange a tidy-up session. The short answer was 'No', and the vicar's godliness seemed to disappear for a few seconds. He looked over his glasses and made it plain that as a non-member of his church, my interference would not really be welcomed. I never expected a church to be such a closed community, and I left the vicarage feeling let down, and, for a while anyway, against all things Yorkshire. Perhaps it was the cold air up there, but I sensed I would have received a warmer welcome in little Barming's churchyard.

I don't know why, but I generally kept quiet about being a keen listener to the Jimmy Young programme on BBC Radio 2. The 'JY prog' wasn't all about recipes, fresh food and 'legal eagles'. (I still had three of my own at that time). I heard JY talk about a scheme that the Thatcher government had thought up, to reduce unemployment. People could be paid to do voluntary work in the community, rather than sit at home doing nothing. I thought of the churchyard, and a few phone calls later I made contact with Volserve, an existing group in Sheffield. Tidying up the churchyard could easily be within their newly created remit, but first I had to clear it with the vicar.

There was a wrong to put right, so I drove up to Sheffield to see him again. He frowned as he opened the big wooden vicarage door, and frowned again when I told him about Volserve. But then his bearing changed, he became thoughtful for a few seconds before promising to, 'put the idea to the committee.' We were in the right place for an alleluia moment, and this was it. He even said he was grateful, though swiftly added that, it would be an entirely in house matter, with which I would not be involved. Such, it seemed, were the ways of the Church. At least I'd made headway, and three weeks later I was delighted to hear from Iris that she'd seen a Volserve sign in the churchyard, bonfires burning and a big difference being made. A difference that remained, because cleanliness still sits next to godliness at Ecclesall churchyard in Sheffield.

As the summer of '84 began, Jackie had left and I had my house all to myself. The villagers of West Chiltington seemed very sociable and my vest emblazoned with 'Love thy neighbour' that I'd worn for the last fun run and while jogging round the village, seemed to go down well. I thought perhaps too well, when a married woman living just up the road volunteered to clean my house for me free of charge.

She arrived armed with dusters and polish and cleaned the house from top to bottom while her ninety-year-old mother played the piano. Things escalated, and one day when my father was visiting she brought down lunch for us both. We sat under the sunshade while lunch was served on silver trays with wine alongside in silver goblets. All the while her mother played the piano. As grateful as I was for a clean house and a good lunch I knew I had to calm things down, so tactfully, (I hope), I stopped the visits. A few weeks later she was spotted running naked around the golf course, so I probably ended our association just in time.

Seeing my clean house prompted me to get a weekly cleaner and that's how I met Collette, though she didn't much seem like a Colette, with her headscarf, a fag-end hanging out of her mouth and a broad East London accent. Her son was in and out of prison and she worked very hard to keep her family together. I thought she was wonderful and we got on like a house on fire, which it could well have been if I'd allowed her to carry on smoking indoors. When she had any news to tell me, which was often, she would wave me across to her and start with ''ere Alan …'. I liked her immensely, and I looked forward to her Tuesday morning cleaning sessions, and to the gossip.

Every couple of weeks my father, still in the doldrums after the death of my mother, drove to see me. He was now the nominated next of kin for my British Airways concessionary travel tickets, and when I was invited to Sydney I was surprised but delighted when he accepted my invitation to come with me. The invite was from Alan and Margaret, our first neighbours from when we were living at Little Spring in Chesham; now they were in Wahroonga, a suburb of Sydney. It would be my father's first venture abroad, at the age of 74, and with a brand new passport in his hand we met at Heathrow Terminal 3.

Incredibly at the very last minute, my two staff tickets turned into first class seats, an icing on the cake if ever there was one. My father made copious notes in his diary from the minute we boarded the flight until we landed back at Heathrow two weeks later. Everything he saw, and everything he heard he wrote down, and I never saw him asleep on the flights.

He was overwhelmed but puzzled that Alan and Margaret made us so welcome, incredulous that two 'strangers' could treat us so well. I thought back to my childhood, when anybody outside the immediate family was a 'stranger' and treated suspiciously. Alan and Margaret looked after us, and we had ten full days, including a trip into the blue mountains and, for me a highlight, a chance to stand outside the Sydney Cricket Ground. We came back rejuvenated, and my father with his notebook filled on every page, ready for my sister to type out and make into a little book. He called it *Flying Jack to Jacaranda*, remembering the purple trees that so impressed him.

We later had holidays together to France and Jersey, but the adventure my father enjoyed the most of all was a long there-and-back flight from Gatwick to Dalaman in Turkey. That was because I was the captain of the Boeing 767, and his seat was right behind me in the cockpit. Events like that gave me special satisfaction, because they wouldn't have occurred without the accident. Those entries on the credit side of the ledger, offset, if only in a small way, the much longer list on the other side.

When I got back from Sydney, the Miami news from Alistair wasn't encouraging. My lawyers had just discovered, after more than a year on the case that the franchisee they were suing was already bankrupt, and had been so for two years.

'Are they competent?' I asked Alistair. 'They know what they are doing,' came his stock reply, so I needn't have asked.

Years later a letter came to light, written by lawyer S in April 1984, in which he said he knew 'Nothing about bankruptcy'. The following month Lawyer S said to the judge, 'Bear in mind if our case goes to a fraud issue… please advise me how to do it.'

It is disquieting to read the letter now, but I guessed it then. I was stuck, paying stage payments to people that I already doubted. I couldn't see how lawsuits, wrongly dated, against a bankrupt company and its insurers could possibly succeed. I agreed with the advice I'd been given by the British Franchise Association, in that we should follow, in their words, a 'well-worn path' against the parent company. But Alistair thought the Miami lawyers were on the right track, and he should know. In any case it was too late to change horses.

The case dragged on, with me thinking that our conversations in Miami had been rushed because of the statute deadline, which seemed to make Alistair's input not only too little but too late. The legal documents I came across much later show that my misgivings were right. I had employed two lawyers, but the correspondence clearly shows that Lawyer S, the junior partner, did almost all the work. He often asked a lawyer from outside the company for advice, starting immediately after the lawsuits were issued. He was told, *'We will have a tough row to hoe against the insurance company, and our course of action would seem to be against the leasing company for not knowing what was adequate insurance, and for not providing it.'* My case exactly.

I'd put those exact thoughts forward at the first meeting at our lawyers' office in Miami, and many times thereafter. Alistair had put it much more clearly in his case notes taken at the time; *'They (Dollar) are soliciting for trade at an international airport. They advertise in Europe, they trade in Europe. They should have made it their business to know that many foreign visitors will not have primary cover.'*

Those words summed up what I thought should have been our case; against Dollar, the renters of the car, but not the already bankrupt Dollar franchisee at Miami Airport. It had to be the parent company in California, exactly as the British Franchise Association advised at the time.

The letters seem to suggest that S felt a degree of panic when he discovered (two years after the event) that the Dollar franchisee was bankrupt. He not only asked his senior partner for help but stressed that the discovery *'precluded the issuing of the lawsuits'*.

The accident, Miami, the prosecution and the civil case were the subjects of my nightmares. It was a mess from top to bottom, and although I tried to only consider Miami on good mornings and with a strong cup of coffee in my hand, I was hanging on a cliff.

Something had to happen, and that meant going back to Miami. Surprisingly, Alistair agreed, and he promised to clear his desk for a visit 'after Christmas'.

As before he would ignore the prosecution, but I would not. This time I would go to the very top in Miami's legal enforcement system, I would see the Florida, Miami-Dade State Attorney, Janet Reno.

I couldn't wait.

My wife, Adrienne, remembered she had postcards to send and scurried to the blue post box, laughing as she said that we'd be home weeks before the cards arrived!

'Not being able to sleep last night, my thoughts went to you. I have read several times of a person missing a flight or cancelling and lived? You I am sure would rather had gone with your loved ones. Am sure there is a mission for you, something you will have to fulfil in this miserable world trying to self-destruct before you can join your loved ones. Don't disappoint your family by not taking an active part in life. From a 78yr old that lost many and seen a lot.'

Part four

Many a time I think to seek
One or the other out and speak

16

Early in January 1985 Alistair and I were in Miami for a second time. We had heard nothing in the seven months since being told that progress had stopped because of the bankruptcy. It was already past the time the statute of limitations allowed for filing a lawsuit, so we would be in a difficult position if our lawyers backed out now. Or if we fired them.

Alistair and I entered the plush offices of lawyer B in downtown Miami with questions to ask, but we were greeted with good news. The bankruptcy court had allowed things to proceed once more, and a trial date had been set for July 1985, just four months away. I took that to mean THE trial date, the one spoken about at our initial meeting, the only possible obstacle in the path to success. The lawyers were ecstatically confident then, so perhaps the end was in sight after all.

It was optimism all round. Alistair and I were asked to make depositions ready for presentation before the court. Things were definitely looking up. Everything was couched in legal terms, some of which I didn't understand, but Alistair was nodding as lawyers do, so he obviously understood. I asked why they had opted to sue an already bankrupt franchisee and their rambling, patronising reply didn't satisfy me, but got a nod from Alistair. I began to think it didn't matter, because a trial and the end of the case was imminent. I left our lawyers' offices feeling hopeful, Alistair to return to the hotel and I went to have my eagerly anticipated meeting with Janet Reno, the

State Attorney for Dade County, Florida.

It was my second plush office of the day, but the scale of this one was enormous. Janet Reno was impressive (a few years later she was President Clinton's Attorney General) and obviously held in awe by her staff. She was stern, very tall and very thin, and welcomed me with a warm handshake, 'What can I do for you Mr. Atkinson?'

I'd mentioned the accident in seeking an appointment, but she said she knew about it at the time. She briefly described her background, telling me she had always lived in Dade County and had a house in the Everglades. She led a team of over ninety attorneys but said, 'We don't always win', instancing the failed prosecution of the white police officers in 1980 which led to mass rioting and the deaths of many people. But, she said, 'I can only do my best.'

She seemed surprised and sighed when she heard that Anderson had not been before the courts and was keen to put things right. I'll always remember her parting words, 'Mr Atkinson, I assure you he *will* be prosecuted'. I'd heard similar words from the district attorney, but this time they seemed more genuine, and she seemed more believable. Certainly, Janet Reno was impressive.

The meeting looked to have gone well, but as I walked back to the hotel, I felt just the opposite. I'd been in that same position before. What on earth was I doing here… again? Why did I have to do this? It was surreal as well as inhumane. Four people had died, and I'd been knocking on doors for four years, but nothing had happened. Janet Reno mentioned the police officers; could anybody, black or white, get justice in this country without a rich American lawyer or a posse of television cameras on their side? I didn't want either, just plain and simple justice. I was powerless, clinging on to the hope that the woman at the top, Janet Reno, would do something to resolve the impasse.

I met briefly with Alistair at the hotel before we caught the flight back to London. Perhaps we had achieved something. Alistair and I duly gave affidavits under oath at the US embassy; me to answer questions about events at the car rental counter in 1981, and Alistair about the differences in car insurance between the USA and the UK.

Things were finally happening, and my optimism was only slightly jarred by a letter from lawyer B, asking for the next stage payment of $4500. I wondered to Alistair why they would want $4500 now if their share of a large compensation payment was imminent. His almost automated response was that they knew what they were doing, and I should do as they asked. I demurred from both those ideas. This time, *they* would have to wait, because I was unconvinced.

In my need to forget about Miami, one summer's afternoon I drove down to Steyning to have a nostalgic look at the dream house I never bought, and I noticed people hang-gliding off the South Downs. It looked simple enough, so I signed up with eight others for a week's beginner's course, in my case having to fit it in with my 'proper' flying.

Day one began with jumps attached to the glider from a three-foot bump, and only gradually did the height increase. The second and third days were cancelled because of rain, and I was working on the fourth. I rejoined on day five, relieved that my classmates hadn't advanced much further, and were only jumping from shallow hillocks. By the end of the day though it was time to jump off the highest hill, and it looked a long way down. I was the last to go, and I sat at the top for a while chewing a long blade of grass, wondering if my instructor, a mere speck far below, and now beckoning me down, realised that I'd missed a day of training. I think it was a friend waiting to take a photo that inspired me to jump, but it was a landing that relieved me like no other. I have the photo, but decided I felt far more at home and a lot safer with an engine.

The nervous energy expended on Miami and my hyperactive way of living had made me thinner and fitter, so I joined a squash league. One of my first opponents was Richard, a local Methodist vicar who rode to the squash court on his bike but still beat me before cycling back. We became friends, and occasionally after the game he'd invite me to join him and his family for Sunday lunch.

Now I saw the busy and difficult life of a vicar, especially an empathic one like Richard. His phone rang every few minutes, calls from desperate people seeking advice, help or even just sympathy. His job was truly endless, for little financial reward. Being an airline pilot seemed very simple and straightforward.

At Christmas he gave me a Bible. Inside he wrote, 'With the special message of Jeremiah 29: 11-14, for you personally'. He had underlined words from those verses: *For I know the plans I have for you... plans to give you hope...* Perhaps that was my most lasting Christmas present ever. Though I never became a 'regular', I tucked the Church away as my backstop; it was always there and always would be if anything else big were to go wrong.

Within a few months something else did. In July of 1985, at the age of fifty-one, my brother Derek died of a brain tumour.

He hadn't been ill long, and it was a shock. The third oldest in the family and the most rebellious, he had stood up against my father's belligerence as we grew up. Like me, he wanted a different life to what he saw around him, and in our late-night chats when we slept four to a room, Derek encouraged me to do well at school and escape the humdrum. Make the 'Great Escape' we called it.

Like his two elder brothers, his own education was impacted by the war, and he also left school at fourteen. He trained to be a carpenter, as Jesus had done, although there the resemblance ended. When he married Sheila, he found the confidence to venture forth, and became a civilian carpenter attached to the British Army in Germany.

On paper anyway, Derek and I shared most in common in the family, and perhaps only circumstances stopped us from being closer. Now he was gone, and I was once more at St Margaret's in Barming for a family funeral. A sad day made sadder by the usual family segregations within the congregation, and I sat with Colin and his family thinking that Adrienne's family and then my own family were so very, very, different.

In the small talk afterwards, somebody gave the consensus view that my mother's death eighteen months earlier was due to the stress of my accident. It might have been true, but it didn't cheer me up.

But then, as seemed to always happen, the sun came out, and I heard that my old school friend John Chrystal, and his Swedish wife Elisabeth were coming to England. Connecticut and New York had given them an invigorating zest, and long walks with them over the South Downs, and evenings in Sussex pubs, worked wonders to push yet another funeral into the background.

July 1985 was the time promised for the trial, and I let the month go by without contacting the Miami lawyers or Alistair, not wanting to disturb the deliberations that I hoped were going on. Then I spoke to Alistair, who as usual wasn't perturbed, although I thought he walked a fine line between *not perturbed* and *not interested*. 'These things happen, trials are often delayed.'

By October 1985 I thought our civil case might have been won, but instead, a letter from lawyer B told us that the promised trial wasn't going to happen. There was no explanation, other than our lawyers were now changing tack. They had unearthed another insurance policy held by Dollar which, we were told, 'will offer coverage in your case'. Accordingly, they would switch the name on the lawsuit from *National Insurance* to *The American Insurance Company*. Lawyer S had already been told in the bankruptcy court that he had been using the wrong name for Dollar Rent A Car; it should have been *The North American Marketing Corporation, Inc, d/b/a Dollar Rent A Car*.

After all that they reminded me again that the next stage payment of $4600 was due. A footnote added that the Dollar franchisee named on our lawsuits was not only bankrupt but without assets.

The cancellation of the trial and now the changing of the name on the lawsuits indicated to me that my lawyers were floundering. I was interested in the name change on the lawsuits, in that it made me question the finality of the statute of limitations; could the big parent corporation Dollar be added?

The $4600 was overdue, but I had deliberately waited to see if the trial date turned out to be real. Now their letter had raised more doubts, and I told Alistair to ask some very specific questions. With regard to the statute of limitations and the adding of the parent Dollar, Alistair had the answers; even in UK law, he said, the parent company is not responsible for the wrong-doings of a franchisee, franchisors and franchisees are separate entities. His letter of 18 November 1985 was well-written, and it asked all my questions, except those about the inclusion of the parent Dollar. Albeit couched in legal terms, he indicated the areas in which, 'Alan would like reassurance'.

Once again, he ended his letter with the usual, 'Sorry to trouble you' adding that his letter was 'probably a public relations exercise,' (which I interpreted as meaning to placate me.) They were platitudes I strongly disagreed with and once again, I wondered if his concerns were very different to mine.

Interestingly, after saying in his letter that I was getting together the $4600, he revealed a doubt he had never voiced to me: He wrote, 'If we are going to lose this case, it would be preferable to face up to the reality now rather than involve Alan in substantial further legal expenses.' At my request he said we wanted to visit them for a third time.

Alistair's letter received no reply, and 1985 dragged in to 1986 with everything hanging in the air. As far as the civil case went, I'd just about given up, and I didn't intend to pay another dollar until I saw the Miami lawyers. In the meantime, I hung on to the thought that perhaps they did sort of know what they were doing, and an announcement of victory would come. But as always, I wasn't holding my breath.

Despite her promise I'd heard nothing from Janet Reno, and

once again I'd almost given up, assuming that a prosecution without my input had taken place and I hadn't been told. Even a phone call seemed pointless; I'd be passed from extension to extension and get nowhere. I couldn't think of anything else to do, and my legal advisor just wasn't interested. Members of Parliament, the Foreign Office, the district attorney and the state attorney had all led nowhere. It seemed there was nowhere else to go.

17

I still had a job to do, and the beginning of 1986 was unusually busy with flights to both northern and southern Europe. Miami was always there, in the background, or very much to the fore when I wasn't flying or being overactive.

Once I wrote to lawyer B, this time bypassing my legal advisor, who still had no reply to his own letter. My letter wasn't couched in Alistair's legal language, neither did it have his terms of endearment, but this time lawyer B replied almost immediately, to say that the newly found insurance policy provided one million dollars to cover the company's negligence, but the problem was interpreting it, and that was being decided by the courts. We just had to wait. While we waited, I withheld the $4600. (Later I discovered that the judge decided *against* the relevance of the new policy, and lawyer S once more engaged specialist lawyers to appeal.)

In the spring British Airways circulated a letter headed, 'Fancy a change?' asking for volunteers to fly the Hawker Siddeley HS 748 twin-engine turboprop aircraft. It would be for eighteen months, based in West Berlin. In my hyper-active state, I sought change everywhere, so I applied, though without much thought, because it was already past the closing deadline. There obviously weren't many applicants, because my name was quickly pencilled in, and I was given a starting date.

The attraction for me was West Berlin, and to fly the air corridors set up after the war to cities such as Munster, Hanover and Bremen. The drawback was the plane, which was ten steps backwards from the Boeing 737 that I'd been flying for six years from Gatwick. It was noisy, slow, too hot in the summer and too cold in the winter.

On many routes at that time, we had a captive clientele who had little choice but to fly with us. Better planes from other airlines sat beside us outside the terminals, and I often saw disappointment on passenger faces as they walked out of the building to board not the shiny Boeing 737 parked next door, but our antiquated propeller HS 748. Some passengers might even have thought that a 748 would be one step better than a 747, but it certainly wasn't!

It was only for eighteen months and was definitely a change. The flying came in blocks, with a few days in Germany followed by a few days at home, and that was another plus.

Just before I moved from Colin's house, I had taken his daughter to Emsworth on the south coast for a week to learn to windsurf. I hadn't done any windsurfing since, so on one 'off' period, I flew down to Corsica to practice in warm water.

On the very first day I met another beginner, there with his wife, and while she sunbathed, we windsurfed. We set up a mid-morning routine to surf up and down the coast. One day we went further than normal and signalled to each other that it was time to divert to the beach for a rest. It looked deserted and it was, except for exactly the point where we made landfall. We jumped off our boards right next to two ladies who were sunbathing naked. It really was by accident that we'd ended up there, but they obviously didn't think so, and shouted loudly at us, luckily using words that were far beyond my 'O' Level French of 1959. We got the message, and surfed from that beach faster than we had come in.

I had hired a car in Corsica and deliberately chose Dollar. I noticed their high profile and fully functioning Dollar Rent A Car desks, and I thought of the recent letter from lawyer B, telling us that Dollar was without assets. They had obviously chosen the wrong Dollar.

Perhaps some of our happiest family times had been our annual two weeks in Fréjus, in the South of France. That part of the world was to me, everything that Florida wasn't, and the more contact I had with Miami, the sharper the contrast became. For the moment, anyway, I was stuck with the rough; the smooth was the south of France. A small flat somewhere on that south coast of France would be my perfect refuge.

Word must have got around, because I was introduced to Catherine, a friend of Bill's daughter, Becky, and originally from Bordeaux. With her husband she managed a wine shop in nearby Pulborough, but as a sideline Catherine sold properties along the length of the south of France. I was a potential customer, so I joined her the next time she went 'down south' to add properties to her portfolio.

We met at Aix-en-Provence, and drove eastwards along the coast towards Cannes, looking at properties ranging from fantastic chateaux to ramshackle stone shacks all with the backdrop of the sun, the sea, and the open space of Provence. It was just good to be there, and the idea of buying some-thing almost slipped into the background. That was until we came to Mandelieu-La-Napoule, an unspoilt commune on the Mediterranean coast about ten miles southwest of Cannes.

Just inland, on the River Siagne, a new marina was almost complete. The already finished giant tower blocks around the edge looked as ordinary as the low-rise apartments being finished looked unique. They were on Ile de Cannes Marina, a finger of reclaimed land stretching out into the Siagne, and each new apartment came with its own mooring.

I was enchanted by it all, and after walking through the building site and looking at a model of how the finished marina would look, I surprised myself and my host, by agreeing to buy, off plan.

At the time, I was impulsive about most things, but that buy was something I never regretted, and it became my escape from everything for the next fifteen years. Only once in all those years did I venture close to the campsite at Fréjus that held so many happy memories. Only briefly, and I shouldn't have, because I was instantly overwhelmed by it all. Those emotions were best left as they were.

Throughout the summer of 1986, nothing was heard from Miami, and we just waited to learn whether the courts would accept, on appeal, the $1 million insurance policy. The next letter, from lawyer S, in November, asked for an extra $500. Without that, he threatened, the appeal could not proceed. That fell on deaf ears; I hadn't sent the $4600 and I wasn't going to send anything until I knew what the situation really was, and that meant yet another visit. Alistair was busy and I think irritated that I wasn't paying our lawyers what they asked, so I arranged to return to Miami by myself for an update.

On 16 December 1986 I arrived at Miami International Airport for my third visit to the city I never wanted to see again. In almost seven years I'd heard nothing from the Miami police, so there seemed little point in another visit to the Miami attorneys, but I made an appointment anyway.

Now for the second time I was in the offices of the District Attorney for Miami-Dade County, and surprisingly he had news. Anderson, he told me, had indeed been prosecuted and had been sentenced to community service.

I asked what that meant, 'Well', he said, 'It *should* mean, as it says, doing unpaid work around the community.' Then without prompting he added, 'He probably didn't do it because it was nobody's job to check that he did'. It seemed to be said in a spirit of frustration, that the law in Miami wasn't followed as it should be.

That was it. In effect nothing, and nobody had cared enough to even inform me of that minimal result. Even after a journey of four thousand miles, made three times, it was obvious that an individual without an army of cameras behind him, couldn't shake the ways of the system. The stark, 'Mr. Anderson has been prosecuted' was apparently enough for somebody like me, and now they couldn't even show me anything to prove a court appearance. Which left the very obvious question, 'Was Anderson ever prosecuted at all?' A question without an answer even now.

Convinced that I'd been fobbed off by the DA deliberately to bring an end to my quest for justice in the criminal court, my only avenue now was to get somewhere in the civil case.

I wasn't in the best of moods as I approached the office of my two lawyers. How I came across, I didn't really care, because I never appreciated Lawyer B's smooth confidence and I really couldn't imagine Lawyer S as a lawyer at all.

I went through my questions, and they listened. *Wasn't the bankruptcy unearthed too late? Were Dollar still trading despite the lack of assets? Were we suing the wrong Dollar?*

Lawyer B gave seamless legal answers about the bankruptcy which I doubted but, *(without then having the paperwork)* I had to accept. It was his answer to my last question, about changing target, which surprised and interested me. He now seemed to think that to change from the minnow-long-bankrupt outlet at Miami International Airport to the mighty Dollar Rent A Car based in California was a possibility. He asked lawyer S to look into it, and to me that was a big step forward, though years too late.

Meanwhile, I was told, our case was going to yet another appeal, this time about the viability of an insurance policy (hardly a reward for almost four years of litigation), which *should,* they said, be finalised by the following summer. For the umpteenth time, they were confident of winning. Inevitably they asked about the $4600, but I said that I would sort something out after I had thought about our meeting, and especially about the matter that Lawyer S was looking into.

Once again, I couldn't wait to jump on the plane and leave Miami, hopefully for the very last time. In truth, despite having a high-flying volunteer legal advisor who was closely linked to the family, it had been a one-man campaign on all fronts. Sadly, I finally admitted, Alastair had neither the time nor the heart for my case. A long and difficult journey had led nowhere. To me, both cases seemed simple; the culprits were Mr. Anderson for causing the accident and Dollar for not even offering the insurance that an American driver would automatically have; or at least telling me that I wasn't covered against all those uninsured drivers on the roads of Florida when I'd asked, 'Am I fully covered?' Yet I had lost the first argument and seemed certain to lose the second. It was always going to be complicated because it had happened thousands of miles away from home. It was always going to be emotionally difficult because I had lost my wife and three children. But I expected to do better than this, and that was very depressing.

I had now travelled three times, 10,000 miles back and forth to the USA, in order to have just ten minutes with the state attorney, two short conversations with the district attorney, a fruitless conversation with the Miami police and to pursue further doomed activity by my legal team. I was alone and I was exhausted.

I got off the plane at Heathrow thinking enough was enough. I would extricate myself from Miami after confirming where we stood on the one legal point upon which I had differed throughout from my legal team. Did we have the wrong name on the lawsuits, and was that why the case was about to fail?

To be sure of my ground, I contacted the British Franchise Association once more, and they repeated their advice given four years earlier; 'Always include the top of the pyramid'. They quoted again the case in New York of O'Boyle v Avis Rent a Car, and the phrase 'A well-worn path'. I sent that information to Lawyer S, who took nine months to reply.

Once home, I thought about the money I supposedly owed. I believed the case was going to fail, and I particularly didn't like the request from S for that extra $500; it seemed they were just trying to get as much as they could, while they could. Alistair said I should pay everything they wanted. We disagreed, not for the first time but certainly for the last time, as that was his last act as my legal advisor.

I had sent off the information from the British Franchise Association to Lawyer S, and if the name on the lawsuit *could* be changed, then I thought there was a chance. I sent off a compromise payment in January 1987, suspecting it was good money after bad.

18

I came from Kent but my love was now Yorkshire; it began by meeting Adrienne from Sheffield and was firmly cemented by our very short spell in Thirsk. Now the bond became even stronger through my regular visits to Ecclesall graveyard, and I felt driven to start living in or around Sheffield. Change was now part of my DNA, as I attempted to continuously shift my focus away from what had happened and still hadn't really come to terms with. Perhaps I sought the promised land foreseen in those personal words from the squash-playing vicar in the Bible which he had gifted me; whatever it was, I was suddenly anxious to move, and everything pointed to Sheffield. It was just across the Pennines from Manchester and its airport, so from there I could go to Berlin and continue flying the HS 748.

I quickly found a small but ideal apartment in just the right place, on the west side of Sheffield. Within a couple of months, I had sold my house in West Chiltington and moved from Sussex to South Yorkshire. On the May morning that I moved in, snow fell against the window, reminding me that I'd moved back up north. However, it was still very good to be back in Adrienne's part of the world.

A British Airways stewardess and her husband lived in Holmfirth, not far from Sheffield, and had a tennis court. Every Thursday night in summer friends were invited to play, finishing with wine and fish and chips. I met Les, an architect from Boston Spa, and we began a lifelong friendship, with many hours flying a Socata Trinidad light plane which he co-owned at nearby Sherburn Airfield. With me doing the flying and Les navigating, operating the radio and twiddling the knobs, we did a two-week tour of France.

Flying was now in my blood, whether working or not. The idea of flying Concorde came suddenly and literally out of the blue. I had just flown into Heathrow from Berlin and had a couple of hours to wait before flying to Manchester. I watched Concorde approach to land, the noise setting off most of the alarms in the car park. It looked as beautiful as the 748 was ugly, as fast as the 748 was lumbering, and once again my mind was racing.

I was contracted to eighteen months on the 748 and that was almost finished, so I wandered round to the office of Captain John Cook, the Concorde training manager, thinking on the way about what I would say. By the time I knocked on his office door I had a script ready in my mind, though perhaps worthy of Enid Blyton. I enthused about the plane, about how much I wanted to fly it, all the while emphasising my RAF training, because I knew that would go down well; he was ex-RAF himself. John was a kind friendly man, and I enjoyed meeting him. As I left his office I paused by the big model of Concorde there and wondered if I would ever fly the real thing.

Less than a month later, I got the news I'd been waiting for; I'd been selected for the Concorde training course.

It was a milestone, as important to me as getting my eleven-plus results on my birthday in March 1953. I got the same sort of indifferent feedback from my family, just the usual, 'Oh yeah, that's nice!'

I was delighted to think that just five months later, in

December 1987, I would finish flying the 748 in Berlin and instead begin the Concorde course in Bristol. I would go from the slowest to the fastest plane in the British Airways fleet.

I was on a high, feeling that I could deal with anything, so I thought I would write to lawyer B. His prompt reply brought no news, saying that due to a large volume of work, no decision would be made for another six months. A month before, that would have worried me, now I was relieved, because I could start thinking and reading about the exacting Concorde training. At the same time, I could settle in to my new home in Sheffield and commute to Berlin for my last few weeks flying the 748. Peace didn't quite come, because out of the blue I got an extraordinary letter from lawyer S. He was obviously stung by my criticisms at our meeting the previous December about the viable franchisor in California being included in the lawsuits. It had taken him over a year to get up a head of steam, and his letter was definitely steamy.

To include the franchisor wasn't possible he said, 'Because there was no representation by the franchisor when you hired the car.' He elaborated; 'We could not have sued the giant Dollar Rent A Car in California because when you hired the car you had no particular reason for choosing Dollar other than they were the first rental agency you saw at the terminal.'

That letter was a long time coming, but it seemed to have been written in haste. As grounds for not suing the mighty Dollar I found his arguments extraordinary; I chose Dollar because I knew the name and had used them the year before in San Francisco. They were a well-known brand and I felt a lot safer hiring from them than from any Fred Smith Rentals that might have been alongside. There, to my mind, lay the link between me and the parent company in California.

His letter finished with an astonishing contradiction. After rubbishing the whole idea of including the franchisor, he said to include them now was *probably impossible* but if I wanted that I should contact him immediately, 'Because time is of the essence.' He had taken almost two years to reply to my suggestion!

My reply to Lawyer S came as quickly as my pen would write. There was representation by the parent company when I hired the car, because their well-known international trademark had been splattered all over the counter! And yes, I did want the franchisor added to the lawsuits.

That brought a bombshell reply; not the one I expected after his letter of one month before. He now said, 'If you want that done, you will have to get another lawyer.'

I had run out of energy to continue the fight on my own. It was totally against my character to give up, but now I had no alternative but to let things in Miami grind to their inevitable conclusion with no input from me. I was about to begin a very long and complicated training course which required my full attention and where failure for me was not an option. I did reply to lawyer S's odd letter, saying that I didn't want to change lawyers at this stage and would wait for the result of the appeal. I would see them for the fourth and very last time, but not until the course was behind me.

The unique intensity of the Concorde course coming up made me take a long hard look at myself and the life I was leading. For seven years I had coped as best I could in the only way I knew how. I had 'boxes' to hold my memories, all the good stuff, to be opened only on the right day and only at the right time. I had 'distractions' to keep my mind occupied, buying houses, then selling them, acquiring things then giving them away. But the intensity of the Concorde course would add another dimension to my life, and something had to give. For the moment anyway, I carried on my unfocused existence, but the strains of Miami would have to end soon.

Getting seriously interested in another woman was always going to be difficult, as throughout my life. Adrienne, Nigel, Anna-Jane and Lucy-Claire, (and even Sophie our dog), were a package that in my mind went together, or not at all. I would find it as difficult to accept another woman without those three children as it was to accept children without Adrienne. There was an indelible line.

The first woman to get seriously close was Christine, a British Caledonian stewardess from Glasgow. The Scottish accent to me was a great plus of course, and the fact that she had no children to compare with my own precious three. But even above all that she was lovely and wonderful to be with. She understood and accepted my hang-ups, and I invited her to Sheffield to meet my 'other world', which was a tall order for both of us. I wondered what Iris would think, as the arch-ally of Adrienne and the custodian of her inner thoughts. How would Christine react to seeing the grave and the effect it still had on me? Perhaps most of all, what would my family think if they looked at her as a replacement for Adrienne?

There was a lot of tension in my already mixed-up mind, but Christine passed 'the test' well, and was liked by all who met her. As for my deepest thoughts about what my family would think; perhaps that's where a good counsellor could have worked wonders, because the concept of a replacement for Adrienne was something I always found difficult to contemplate.

The Concorde training was to last six months, double the length of any other flying conversion course. Rather than drive down from Sheffield, I stayed with Christine, at her house in East Grinstead.

The first three months of the course were at Bristol, where the plane was built, and involved learning about all the technical systems, which was followed by long sessions on the flying simulators. My new plane had four times as many systems as a conventional plane, which explains why the course was so long. A few days on electrics, then hydraulics, then pneumatics… and so it went on.

After spending the weekend trying to fix everything into my brain, I drove down from Sussex every Sunday night and returned exhausted late on Friday. Once fed, watered and refurbished each weekend, I was sent back to Bristol on Sunday night all polished up and raring to go. The ground school finished with a lengthy exam which had to be passed, and which was so long and so involved that it was really a test in memory retention.

Next came two-hour sessions on the flight simulator. These were also intense, with four simulator hours spent just learning the Concorde's low-noise departure from New York; the powerful anti-Concorde lobby in the state meant strict adherence to noise levels. Everything was timed to the second, the reheats for the four big Rolls-Royce Olympus engines going on, then off precisely, with exact changes in speed and height as well as angle of bank. Precision was essential because after each Concorde take-off from JFK Airport Air Traffic would pass a decibel read-out, and, if it was over the limit (and because of the temperature, wind or air pressure it sometimes was) British Airways would receive a hefty fine.

The last phase of the course was the best, the flying. In an empty and therefore very light and lively Concorde we flew 'circuits and bumps' at Prestwick in Scotland and Shannon in Ireland. Those airfields were wisely chosen for what we were doing, because they had long runways and relatively few people living close by to complain about the noise. However much they rehearsed it in the simulator, every new pilot's first Concorde take-off caught them by surprise. We were supposed to level-off at 2500 ft, but the acceleration was such that unless you cancelled the reheat and retarded the throttles just after lift-off you were already past that height. One circuit used 3.5 tons of fuel.

In May of 1988 I had finished the course and was rostered to fly as co-pilot on my first passenger flight to New York. The routine was that the flight crew (two pilots and flight engineer) met at one of the Heathrow hangars, instead of the main building, before being driven to the briefing room, and then about an hour before takeoff, to a plane that usually hadn't flown before that day. The pre-flight checks were lengthier than I'd known, but one of the many gems of flying Concorde was a packet of digestive biscuits and a mug of tea sitting beside the seat when you entered the cockpit.

Every scheduled Concorde flight was about three hours and twenty minutes, during which we reached 60,000 feet and spent over half that time at twice the speed of sound. On my third flight to New York the weather worsened as we got closer, and we had to divert to Windsor Locks Bradley International Airport in Connecticut, to wait until the weather improved.

Connecticut was where a lot of our passengers lived, and there were murmurs from some of them about leaving the plane and going home. That would have created all sorts of problems, but luckily the weather in New York improved quite quickly and we resumed our journey.

We had regular customers to New York and they frequently came into the cockpit. One, an amateur pilot as well as CEO of a real estate company in New York, liked to stay for the landing. With the engines shut down, we three in the cockpit accepted his offer of a lift to Manhattan in his helicopter. He sat next to the pilot and we three sat in the back for the short flight across the East River, grateful to miss the usual long journey on the deadlocked roads. Waiting for our helicopter was a big black limousine, and again we sat in the back while our host answered constant quick-fire questions from his PA. When the car stopped, outside a very imposing building our all-action man bounded up the steps, ready to speak to the assembled throng. We were all impressed; he hadn't had a quiet moment for the last four hours and was now making a speech. We could understand how some of our passengers could afford to go backwards and forwards on Concorde.

One of the scheduled routes for Concorde was to Washington, and then on to Miami, the last place on earth that I wanted to go to. To ask not to go there, besides causing havoc in the flight rostering department, would have risked crossing that dividing line I tried to keep between my emotions and work. But my fourth scheduled Concorde flight was indeed to Miami and I stayed in my room for the brief fifteen hours we were there. I was pleased to fly the sector out, onwards to Washington, and got great pleasure from powering away from that Florida coastline, though I did look once and wonder where it all happened.

But then, with a few flights under my belt, it was time to arrange one final visit to Miami. I'd heard nothing from my lawyers, but I didn't really hope for anything because of my workload on the course, or expect anything, because in my head I had already written them off. The only option that I thought might be possible (and it would bring mental compensation to me if nothing else), was to sue my two lawyers for negligence, because it seemed to my non-legal mind that their handling of the case had been shambolic from day one. Alistair was no longer involved, but anything along those lines was bound to be steeped in legal jargon, and I asked a solicitor friend, Alistair Cree, to come with me for support. In September 1988, we arrived in downtown Miami; it was my fourth and surely my last visit, seven-and-a-half years since the accident.

I went to lawyer B's office alone, not because I thought another Alistair might confuse him, but because it would take ages to bring Alistair 2 into the loop. Just Lawyer B was there, and the two of us took turns to speak to Lawyer S on the phone. Lawyer B, the senior partner was in the real world, had already confirmed that we were coming to the end of the road, whereas Lawyer S spoke as if there was still everything to play for; we just had to wait for the result of the latest appeal.

Once again, I recited the wisdom to Lawyer B of including the franchisor on the lawsuits and he seemed interested. He said he would put the idea to lawyer S, forgetting that he had said the very same thing two years earlier. I asked yet again why they had taken out a lawsuit against a bankrupt company, and he said that a search would not have revealed the bankruptcy.

I wondered aloud about that, because I just didn't believe it.

I left his office with copies of the legal documents knowing full well that this was the end of an error-strewn saga. It was a breath of fresh air to discuss it with Alistair Cree. This had to be my last visit to Miami, so a case for negligence against my lawyers would have to be put in motion now, and that wouldn't be easy. The planned three days might not be enough, but I didn't want to stay longer or ever return to the place.

We scouted around Miami looking for a lawyer who would take up the case. It was a difficult proposition in a closed-shop city, made almost impossible because we were cold calling every office we went to. We needed more time and some contacts but we had neither; those Americans would hardly say hello without presenting an invoice, let alone give free information. After seven years the American legal system was getting on my nerves, and I'd lost respect for the people I was having to meet. However, at the very end of our visit, we found one lawyer who agreed to look at our paperwork, and we left it with him before we returned home. Explaining the case was never easy, because in parochial USA they couldn't really grasp the concept that any system of insurance could be different to their own.

That summed up the whole sorry expensive saga. I don't know whether we hadn't been able to explain the 'insurance black hole' sufficiently well, or the lawyers we'd chosen had simply erred in barking up the wrong tree, so it was more in hope than expectation that I sent Alistair M's earlier comprehensive press release and other information explaining our insurance system to one lawyer who showed intertest, but deep down I suspected it was all a waste of time. Sure enough, a week or two later I received a letter saying simply that we might have a case but he didn't want to take it on.

That was the end of both the civil case and my long search for a prosecution. At that point my family were still very fresh in the minds of friends and relations and it would have been the ideal moment to produce a memorial truly fitting and lasting for their memory. I hoped for a permanent bursary in their names at Glasgow or Sheffield University linked to special educational needs children. But now that hope was gone. After all the efforts, the trips back to the one place I never wanted to see again, the promises from right, left and centre, my wonderful family had gone far too quietly, without even the marker of a proper prosecution. They deserved better and I felt ashamed. Others should have done too. I'm sure there was a path to what I wanted and the justice my family deserved; in hindsight I should have employed a good lawyer in the UK before choosing the two in the USA. To do that now meant starting again and I had my sanity to think about. I decided that I must get on with my life.

I received a final letter from lawyer B. We had lost the appeal. He also confirmed what I had long suspected: it was the junior partner, lawyer S, who had handled my case. That probably explained it all.

The usual destination of Concorde was New York; it was there one day and back the next, departing London at breakfast time or early afternoon. I thought that commuting to Heathrow either the night before or during the morning from my flat in Sheffield would be reasonably easy. It was, except that the quietness of the MI on my commute back at 1 am encouraged me to go faster, and I got two speeding tickets in a month. Winter commuting wasn't really reliable enough, so after a couple of long motorway delays and those speeding tickets I started to think about moving closer to Heathrow.

I tested the water by renting a basement flat in Kensington for three months, and soon discovered that life in the big city wasn't as sedate as in my beloved Yorkshire. I had my car stolen the second week, and not long after discovered that my Argentinian landlady liked to bypass the electric meter with wire and magnets. It was time to move, preferably somewhere closer to Heathrow.

I bought a small studio flat overlooking the Thames at Barnes, almost on the finish line for the University Boat Race, which was scheduled for the following month. My neighbours above and alongside were planning boat race parties, so I decided to do the same and it became an annual event. I invited just about everybody I knew and some I didn't really know; four of my guests at my first party spent the whole race at the party upstairs, drinking their wine and eating their food, before realising they were in the wrong flat.

By now I was free of Miami and hooked on to a frenetic ever-changing lifestyle, aiming to use the proceeds from my house in Sussex to buy small bolt-holes in the places that I had seen on my BA travels and liked best. I already had the studio flat in France, and now one in London, so I began to think about Cape Town, in South Africa.

On my next visit I focused on a small estate of almost finished new apartments, tucked up high underneath Signal Hill and overlooking the vast new Waterfront development. I didn't make my mind up to buy until two days before I had to fly back to London, but I didn't mention that deadline until I had shaken hands on the deal with the Jewish agent from

Sambell Estates, and that created a problem; I would have to sign the contract the next day but it was a very religious day in the Jewish calendar. The agent was sorry, but he definitely couldn't work or be seen to be working on that day, so sadly the deal was off.

The next afternoon I got a hushed phone call, and I knew who it was from. 'Meet me on the corner of Beach Road and Marais Road in half an hour.'

Sure enough, my agent was there, covered from head to toe to disguise his appearance in case he saw someone he knew, but with the contract and a pen in hand. He didn't actually say, 'Business is business my boy,' but the deal was done, and I owned another small flat in a lovely part of the world. It wasn't yet finished, and I knew I wouldn't be returning for a while, so I found an agent to rent it unfurnished. When I did move in two years later the neighbours were delighted to see me, because the tenant was one of Cape Town's many drug dealers.

Flying Concorde trumped most things, and it didn't matter that I lived in a small apartment or that most of my furniture was once more sitting in store. London felt vibrant and sat well with my peaceful refuge in France and the one being completed in Cape Town. I'd found my niche, Miami was off the radar and I hoped to return to a more settled life.

19

Living in Barnes made life simple; in forty minutes I could be at the airport and five hours later in New York or Washington. Concorde had a crew of nine, two pilots and a flight engineer and six cabin crew headed by a Cabin Service Director in the 100-seat cabin. I was now at the beginning of a particularly long process to get from co-pilot to Concorde captain. This would take seven years as copilot, then three years as a captain on another plane, before I could apply to be a captain on Concorde. I was happy with that, or almost, because the flying was unique and all the flying, take-offs and landings were shared between the two in the front two seats. For the first few weeks that meant that I was at the controls to either New York or back.

In the beginning flying Concorde was hard work, very different to anything I'd done before, and all-absorbing. But eventually it became, if not routine, familiar and I began to think of other things. In particular of a small boat to sit on the mooring in front of my tiny flat in France.

I went to the Earls Court Boat Show and saw dozens of impressive-looking speedboats, virtually all above my price range. But then one took my eye, and I could just afford it, especially if I exported it immediately to France to avoid the VAT. It was a Bayliner Capri, twenty-two feet long with an inboard engine and a small cabin at the front. I bought it at the Boat Show and collected it at Dover, wrapped in plastic, and on a trailer ready for export. On the quayside with me was my brother-in-law, David and his son, Philip. Their car had a tow bracket, so we hitched up the boat, crossed to France on the ferry and drove down the toll roads to my new little flat in Mandelieu.

Next morning was perfect for the launch, and a maiden voyage. We reversed the trailer towards the slipway, then looked at each other. None of us knew anything about boats, let alone boats with engines. Philip was the youngest, the bravest, and probably the best swimmer, so David and I put his name forward. We looked on incredulously as the boat floated and the engine worked, and in admiration as Philip drove it gingerly along the River Siagne, and then into my mooring. I fastened it tightly with about two miles of rope, just to make sure. Then, with a bottle of champagne, I christened the boat; *Lucy-Anna*, of course.

I needed a car to leave at my new flat, and because it was France that meant a car with character. I spotted a blue Austin Mini-Moke in the supermarket car park, with '*A Vendre*' on a sign in the back window, and I chased after it. The driver was a big jovial Frenchman, so big that the cigar in his mouth was burning a hole in the canvas roof. With a new roof it would be just what I wanted, and he accepted my offer.

The apartment in France with *Lucy-Anna* moored underneath and my Moke in the car park was more than a sunny retreat; it was a bolthole of peacefulness, somewhere to where I could escape. On my days there I had a routine of cleaning the boat in the morning and after stocking up with provisions (French cheese, a baguette, a small bottle of wine, a flask of coffee and yesterday's English newspaper) I'd motor down the Siagne and into the Mediterranean. When well offshore I switched off the engine and drank my wine and ate my French baguette as I drifted back into shore. I thought of nothing and listened to the sea. I spoke to nobody, not even to an irate Frenchman when I ran aground. My schoolboy O' level French didn't seem to work anyway.

With a new-found contentment, I met Hillie, one of the ladies I probably should have married. Gorgeous as well as talented, she was the bundle of infectious fun that I needed. Her house was on the Thames at Chiswick, so henceforth we alternated our boat race parties, though mine on a small flat balcony was outshone by hers on a nice stretch of grass beside the Thames. We gelled completely, and became very close, and for the first time in my 'new life' I allowed myself to get close to a woman's family, even playing in a father/son cricket match at a very posh school in west London. That match ended happily when I carefully aimed a catch to Hillie's son Jamie fielding at mid-wicket, so ensuring that we 'fathers' lost, and Jamie felt very happy with himself and with me. Adrienne had often said that my best talent after wallpapering was being a father.

As one of many sidelines, Hillie was an agony aunt for a woman's magazine, and even wrote a book on 'agonising', adding a dedication at the front of my copy, *To Alan, who I spent so much time agonising with, and over*. She saw the problem I had in releasing myself from my family into hers and booked three appointments for me with a counsellor in Chelsea. I was grateful and, very reluctantly I went, though having developed a way of coping I was unwilling to disturb a hornets' nest of memories and emotions that might send me crashing to earth.

The first session I began tensely, though I did say what I

was there for, and gave an outline of the accident eight years before. The counsellor didn't probe me further, something I was grateful for at the time, but knew missed the point of why I was there. We talked about everything under the sun for those three counselling sessions, and I left with my nest and my problems undisturbed. With my work in the background and so important to me, I just wasn't ready for the risk of counselling. (My next counsellor, in Cape Town almost twenty years late, was much more incisive, and although it hurt at the time, the process was much more beneficial.)

Hillie was multi-talented, with a beautiful singing voice. She produced, sang, and acted in a touring 'Edwardian' revue with top singers and actors of the day including a double act with Barbara Windsor. Barbara was notoriously meticulous at rehearsals, and would often ruffle a few feathers, but Hillie would always calm things down, after Barbara summoned her with ''Ere Hillie, come over 'ere.' I was wary of being centre stage in anything (talking to passengers was for me the most difficult part of flying), but I helped out with the electronics back-stage, plugging in and switching on various leads, always half-expecting a big explosion.

When I was at my very closest to Hillie and, uniquely, her children, I walked away. One bright Sunday morning I awoke with just one thing on my mind, thinking that my lovely sacred link with Adrienne and the children was at risk and I shouldn't allow it. I was a man on a mission, as I walked along the towpath, across the bridge, and back along the path on her side of the Thames. I thought of nothing other than what I had to do.

She answered the door and I blurted out my thoughts and

said my mind was made up. I ignored her and walked back home, but those tears haunted me later. She was a kind, loving woman. *If only,* I thought hundreds of times later about lots of different scenarios. *If only,* for instance, I 'd talked it over with that Chelsea counsellor, and he might have earned his fee by saving me a lifetime of emotional highs and lows, and others a lot of unhappiness.

Ending things with Hillie made me question the veneer I maintained of being able to cope, and I wondered for the first time whether putting my emotions in boxes was leaving its mark on other sides of my life. It was as clear as a bell to me that the accident was too seismic, to 'get over', in part because my mind would never let it slip away. I had to be my family's flag carrier, the custodian of their memory; doubly so, because there had been hardly a whimper from those that mattered. A clear prosecution of Mr. Anderson, or the hoped-for bursary from a successful civil case would have added some weight to the whole matter. I needed a marker that clearly recorded it all, headed by the simple words, 'This happened, and it shouldn't have happened.' Words I expected, and my family deserved; and at the very least that perhaps would have allowed my grief to slide slightly into the background without the need for mental 'boxes'. Who knows, it might have allowed me to let the old and the new live side by side, cured my restlessness and allow me to achieve the only likely panacea of a new family relationship.

A loud clear marker bolstered by good counselling at an early stage could have made a difference, but it seemed that to get the first I needed an army of expensive lawyers or a gaggle of television cameras behind me. Hillie tried her best with the second, to her eternal credit.

17 February was obviously a big date for me and every year so far, I had managed to drive up to the graveyard without asking for that day off. Now flying Concorde, I was not only rostered to fly on that special day but, by a twist of fate, my planned destination was Miami on the eighth anniversary of the accident. It was one of those instances when I looked up to the heavens and asked how it could possibly be. I thought of the words, often quoted to me, and written on the opening page of the Bible given to me by the squash-playing vicar; 'God is working his purpose out.' He was certainly working in mysterious ways, but my problem was solved when my fellow Concorde pilot and good friend Dick Routledge swopped flights, and I went to New York instead.

Flying Concorde into Cape Town, South Africa 18 March 1992

20

The scheduled flights to New York and Washington were interesting, and the week-long stays in Barbados during the winter were the icing on the cake. During my time on the plane, the emphasis began to change from scheduled to charter flights, and almost my last flight on Concorde was to Cape Town, hastily arranged by BMW to celebrate the launch of the 3-series car in South Africa, where the vehicles were assembled. Our flight to Johannesburg was planned to be over the sea most of the way, and therefore supersonic, with our two stops for fuel at Lisbon and Abidjan, on the Ivory Coast.

Abidjan's Port Bouet Airport was a tense place, with armed guards round our plane as we took on fuel, but my lasting memory is the take-off. We used up most of the runway, and as we lifted off, I saw a man pushing his bike across the threshold. He stood transfixed, as we roared just a few feet above his head. This was Africa.

Johannesburg was our base for the week, and every day we flew from there to Cape Town with one hundred BMW-invited passengers, our route taking us over the sea so we could again go supersonic. I flew the first morning's flight to Cape Town, which was perfect for me to make one of my last Concorde landings in the city which had been a big part of my life.

We were asked to make a long, protracted approach to the airfield, so it could all be filmed from a helicopter. On a typically beautiful day we flew along the south coast, passing Cape

Point, Camps Bay and then alongside Table Mountain, before we saw the airfield, the helicopter and then the crowds around the airfield; Concorde was a rare sight in that part of the world.

Next to the terminal, were parked fifty new BMW 3-series cars and two by two, our passengers left the plane and were shepherded into the cars. They were all driven to a wine farm in Paarl for a lunch in the sun, and on the last of the seven days our whole crew was invited to go with them. Every day, in mid-afternoon we flew back to Johannesburg with our satisfied well-fed passengers.

That flight was a perfect finale to my four and a half years flying Concorde. I still think of it as a wonderful plane, for the crews, the passengers and even, eventually for the airline. It was a highly successful centrepiece of British Airways marketing, and at its height(!) those seven Concordes made one quarter of the airline's profits.

But for me it was time to move on. The airline had suddenly expanded, and I had moved up the sacred British Airways seniority list. I could move from right-hand seat to left-hand seat, from co-pilot to captain. My time had come, and I was offered a command, on the Boeing 757 and 767, two planes that were so simple that a captain was licensed to fly both. The conversion course was much shorter and simpler compared to that for Concorde, and in three months I was flying the Boeings from the left-hand seat out of Heathrow and Gatwick.

Both planes were very automated, but the routes were varied, going to more distant places in Europe than I'd been before. Even across the Atlantic now that the engines were deemed reliable enough to allow it, and I spent three weeks in Buenos Aires flying the Boeing 767 with local cabin crew around South

America, which was a part of the world I had never seen.

On a miserable wet and windy day in the centre of Buenos Aires I watched what looked like a mother and daughter huddled under an umbrella, trying to pick out somebody's name from a roll of six hundred on the Falkland Islands War Memorial. It took them time, and they got very wet, but I saw their joy when they found the name they were searching for. In a way, they had succeeded where I had failed, in finding a marker to give some sort of closure to what had happened to their loved one. For them it was a senseless war. For me it was a senseless act on a dark road in Florida.

There was still one plane I needed to fly to complete my own personal ambitions, and that was the biggest of them all, the Boeing 747. It would be another full circle, from the big but lumbering Beverley I had flown in the RAF to the even bigger, but a lot faster jumbo jet of British Airways. So after serving my minimum time on the 767, I applied for a change, and was delighted to see my name down for a Boeing 747 conversion course. I could end my British Airways flying career, with the satisfaction of piloting another plane that I'd always wanted to fly.

Another course later, another box ticked when I flew to New York as the captain of a Boeing 747. I thought the Boeing 767 was for button-pushers and screen-watchers; the Jumbo to me was a real aeroplane, for basic hands-on flying. I loved its sheer inertia, it seemingly had to be coaxed to wallow into the air. The 747 and Concorde were definitely the highlights of my career.

As I began on my new plane, Bill Brennen was about to retire, both from the 747 and from British Airways. I held him in the very highest regard as a boss. but especially for the help he had given me in Miami when I needed it most. His final flight couldn't happen quietly. Just as years before I'd been astonished to find that the RAF had a fleet of large yachts, now I discovered that British Airways had a Scottish pipe band, and they agreed to be there as Bill taxied in his 747 at Heathrow. I'd written, 'Bye-Bye Bill', on a long banner, which was stretched out behind the band. As he taxied in the giant Boeing 747 for the very last time, we had the banner, lots of people, champagne and bagpipes to welcome him. A deserved farewell for somebody who flew the flag well for British Airways and before that, the Fleet Air Arm. For me, of course, he couldn't have done more.

Life for me was on the up and as good as it could be, spending my days between flights living in France, driving my Mini-Moke around the coast or my little boat off it. My only real tie to the UK was Sheffield, and I always tried to be there for birthdays and anniversaries, though one visit gave me a tremendous shock.

I arrived at the graveside to see a massive hole in the ground, an inch or two from my family's grave, and close enough to cause the headstone to tilt. I couldn't stop myself looking down in to that hole, right up against 'my' grave. It was unbelievably shattering; and nothing could be worse.

It was a winter's afternoon in February and there was nobody around, as I ran in a panic to the church and then the sexton's hut. I had to tell somebody, and I called Liz, a dentist friend in Sheffield, but she was with a patient and couldn't come over. For a while I was stunned, and now absolutely certain that I'd chosen the wrong churchyard for my family.

Early the next morning after a sleepless night and still very angry, I phoned the vicar and arranged to see him. He seemed unduly calm about the whole thing, which didn't seem very vicar-like to me. 'Oh', he said 'That hole was made by Heath and Co, the local undertakers, in preparation for their own family vault'. Those words inflamed the whole situation, because *any* undertaker should have known better, but just a few years before I had paid this particular undertaker to create the grave they had just violated.

Sadly, the vicar's words were matter-of-fact, without any appreciation of how distressed I felt, so I left and phoned Heath and Co. I swore for about ten minutes, something they were probably not used to in their line of business. At least they listened, then half-apologised and donated a sum to charity, none of which changed my thoughts about what they had done.

Many years later I met one of the Heath family at the graveside, and got a full apology. We shook hands, acknowledging that we were destined to be neighbours one day, he in the shiny vault and me, with my family, next door.

A big change of scene was always my remedy for sadness so I arranged a holiday in Cape Town. For the first time I would stay in the flat I had bought off plan years earlier and which was now vacated by the drug dealer, albeit having left a mess behind.

Views were everything in Cape Town so when I heard that a new hotel was planned in front of my view of Table Bay, it was time to sell. I employed Peter the painter and he turned up promptly with his small army of helpers to paint just about everything in sight. They finished it beautifully within a week, working long days and only ever stopping for an early fish and chip breakfast and early fish and chip tea. It was impressive, so I asked Peter to lay a small stone patio.

I wasn't there when he drove his old car, towing a trailer full of heavy stones, up the very steep hill to the security gate. A window cleaner later told me what happened next. Peter got out his car to open the gate, but the handbrake didn't hold and the trailer careered down the hill, destroying a new Mercedes at the bottom, luckily without anyone being hurt.

I gave up the idea of a patio, and within a week my flat was sold. I decided that properties just meant work and I wouldn't buy again in Cape Town. That is, until I saw the most perfect apartment on the seafront, with 360-degree views over everything. My flats in London and France were tiny, but this was massive, ideal for my looming retirement. I persuaded myself that Cape Town was the place to retire to, because after all my visits I knew more people there than anywhere else. For once, it seemed, I was thinking ahead, and after the usual haggling I had an apartment on the tenth floor of Thermopolae, Beach Road, Cape Town, which overlooked the sea, the city, a golf course and Table Mountain. Just the place to enjoy retirement.

I got back to London to hear that Auntie Iris had, at the age of 81, died, and that was a big loss. She was closest of all to my wife and children, and virtually indispensable to me after the accident. Only with her could I 'open my boxes' and really share my grief. Our long and close relationship was blighted in her last years by my Miami saga with her son Alistair, a saga that could have brought some sort of closure to both Iris and myself, but instead brought distrust rather than peace. But Iris was one of the giants in my life, and in the short lives of my wife and three children.

Sisters and the best of friends

Our yearly search for conkers with Iris at Chatsworth

£2.3m for the families of death crash sailors

THE families of two car crash victims have been awarded £2.3 million each.

The payment is made under a law which holds car hire firms responsible for accidents involving their cars, regardless of who was driving.

The victims — two British sailors from the Ark Royal aircraft carrier — were killed in a crash in America two years ago.

A third sailor who was injured in the smash was awarded £800,000 by the jury in Miami. The ruling is being seen as a test case for British

Mail on Sunday reporter

tourists injured or killed in the United States.

Passengers David Stark, 34, and David West, 35, died when their hire car driven by 38-year-old John McGreevy, from Plymouth, plunged into a snake and alligator-infested canal in Florida.

Trial

Benjamin Clay, 38, survived but nerves in his face were severed and he still suffers nightmares about the crash. The accident hap-

pened after the four sailors from the Ark Royal hired a car from Alamo Rent-a-car in Fort Lauderdale.

Thirteen witnesses flew in from Britain for the trial at which lawyers originally asked for damages of £2.3 million.

Attorneys Ronald Buschbora and Brett Panter argued in court that under Florida's 1934 'dangerous instrumentality law', Alamo Rent-a-car was responsible for the dead driver falling asleep at the wheel. Other states have similar laws and companies have been held liable in the past.

King's Cr

*'I saw this report in Mail on Sunday and obviously thought about you.
It may or may not be relevant to your circumstances and you
probably follow up these sort of things…
Trust you're enjoying the aeronautics on Concorde.'*

Capt. Pete Smith 737 LGW

Part five

The innocent and the beautiful
Have no enemy but time

21

B ritish Airway's enforced retirement age of fifty-five crept closer, and frustratingly, there was no sign of the company increasing it, as most other airlines had done. Meanwhile, I was happy in the niche I'd found living in La Napoule and flying the 747 from London mostly to the USA or India. Going to the former, I put weight on; going to India I usually lost it, because the food didn't really suit me.

We were once stranded in Delhi for days because of an Air Traffic Control strike. When the strike finished we flew an empty 747 to Bangladesh to pick up passengers desperately waiting to fly down to India. As the passengers boarded, I sat on the flight engineer's seat looking at the departure details, when the page seemed to rotate, I was sick, and then lying on the floor with one of the boarding passengers, a doctor, looking after me. I had food poisoning attributed to the samosas I had eaten on the empty flight from Delhi. Those samosas cost BA a lot of money and exasperated a lot of passengers as the long-awaited flight was delayed, until a replacement captain arrived. I returned to London as a passenger the next day.

I didn't look forward to retirement and my last flight with British Airways, but a consolation was that I could choose my final destination from the ones that we flew. I chose Barbados for obvious reasons, but also because England were due to play a Test match there against the West Indies. We only had two clear days in our hotel, and the match started on the second day. The whole crew amassed at the Kensington Oval cricket ground (there is one in Barbados as well as in London) but as the play started so did the torrential rain! But we all stayed and saw just three hours of play at the end of the day. Even so, as a cricket fan the day ticked off another box in my life as well as providing a souvenir cricket bat signed by all members of the crew. Even better, I got back to Heathrow three days before my birthday and was happy to find that an extra 'final' flight had been rostered for me, this time to Boston.

This was definitely final and made extra special as our 747 climbed away from Heathrow, when I discovered a friend from London, Rolf Kern, was on board having bought a return ticket especially. Already the trip promised to be special because John Buckley, the flight engineer, sitting just behind was coincidentally on his final flight and had his wife sitting beside him in the cockpit for most of the journey. At times like that I missed having someone really close to share it all with, but at least Rolf had done his best to bridge that gap. We all had a great night out in Boston, my favourite of all the cities that I went to in the USA.

Awake early next morning because of the time difference, I prepared a short speech for the expected British Airways reception back at Heathrow. Public speaking was something I had always hated, and I was especially wary of breaching my deliberately maintained wall between emotions and work. As I wrote about leaving, I couldn't help but think about when I joined British Airways, those edgy days when Adrienne and I risked all to give up the pension and security of the RAF for the uncertainty of working for an airline. With that in mind, but not on paper, I prepared what I thought was an appropriate and amusing speech.

As we taxied on to the stand at Heathrow, I could see the British Airways men in suits and a few others waiting. With everything carefully switched off (there could be no mistakes with everybody watching) we all moved to the front of the plane.

I was presented with a framed photograph of the 747 and a bottle of champagne, and then it was time for me to speak. Unfortunately, I couldn't... except for a very inadequate and pathetic, 'Thank you.' Thoughts were buzzing round my head from very many directions and it shames me to say that I didn't say the words I'd prepared so carefully earlier. I think I let down myself, John Buckley, the crew and Adrienne... she would have expected more.

But that was the end of my twenty-five years of flying with British Airways, from the Viscount around the Highlands and islands of Scotland to the Boeing 747 crisscrossing the Atlantic, with Concorde in between. I had met great people inside and outside the aeroplanes, and I was grateful.

I could feel the advantages of being a free man but after just a few days (when I'd signed up for all sorts of wish-list courses like paint spraying and yoga), retirement felt like a big blank canvas with no real reason to go anywhere. Nobody depended on me, and the discipline of having to be somewhere at a certain time had gone. My studio flats in France and London weren't really homes, because most of my belongings (except for Adrienne's baby grand piano which was squeezed into that tiny flat in Barnes) had been in storage, gathering dust for years. I wasn't ready to move to South Africa. Everybody said I needed a base, and I knew that I did, but it was where and when that vexed me. I had too many variables, perhaps too much choice. Yorkshire had drawn me with its magnetic power, ever since those happy days when Adrienne and I lived in the market square in Thirsk, so I drove up there to leave my details with some estate agents.

On the way back, I stopped at the graveyard for my girls' birthday, on 18 April, and as ever thus, it was the place to bring things back to basics and focus my mind. I decided I wasn't ready for a house in Yorkshire, and in the absence of any other anchor point, I would have to find a job. Fingers crossed that I would eventually find the right person to stabilise my life.

Meanwhile being free of work I could reassess all things Miami. The bottom line was that I'd got nowhere, but I couldn't think of anything else I could do. Nobody bothered that justice hadn't been done either in the prosecution that didn't happen nor the shambolic civil case that did. I needed a posse of influence behind me, and a marker for what had happened. Perhaps to write a book would get me both. At the very least, I'd shine a much-needed light on the whole sordid episode.

The accident and the months after were permanently etched in my mind, as were my efforts to get a prosecution. They would be easy to recollect on paper. It was the civil case that had been painful to witness and now would be a problem to write about. It wasn't complicated, even to my non-legal mind, once I saw through the misty veneer of legal speak. It was the timelines in the civil case that I needed to be exact about, and the only place I could find that information was in the batch of legal documents which I thought had been sent to me after my very last visit to Miami. Unfortunately, I had moved several times since then, but hopefully they were somewhere in store. A book would definitely come but after I had found those papers.

Meanwhile, I did what I could do, including flying up to Scotland to meet teachers at the children's school, where I was shown the two 'Atkinson' sports cups, presented at the annual sports day. To see Anna-Jane, Lucy-Claire and Nigel's names engraved on the side was uplifting and emotionally devastating at the same time. I heard teachers who taught my children talk about them so fondly, and so it was a good, if sad visit. Those who were there at the time described the tremendous effect it had on the school, something I was always aware of, though now I saw the actuality and it all hit home.

When I left the school, I went to Helensburgh Swimming Club, the scene of so many family gala nights, cheering Nigel to win as he always did. Now it was to see and discuss the 'Nigel Atkinson Swimming Cup'. That emotionally draining day convinced me that the accident was just too big for me to ever 'get over', and I was in no mentally fit state to retire yet to the emptiness of Yorkshire.

For a while, and fresh from that visit to Scotland, I mulled over the information I had about Miami. I read a *Mail on Sunday* press cutting sent to me by Captain Brian Smith, a colleague at Gatwick, about an accident in Florida that was almost a mirror image of mine, but five years later. Four sailors from the visiting HMS *Ark Royal* had hired a car from Alamo Rent A Car in Fort Lauderdale, and driven across the Everglades. When their car 'tumbled several times' and landed in water, three were killed and one escaped from the submerged car with a badly gashed face.

The hired car, the stretch of road, the tumbling and the one survivor, all had an eerie synchronicity with my accident five years before. Except that this driver fell asleep and was totally to blame. In the same Dade County court where my civil case had spluttered to a halt, the *Ark Royal* case ended with Alamo ordered to pay $7.7 millions under a 1934 state law that holds the owner of a car liable for any accidents regardless of who is driving it.

One quote from the trial sticks in my mind; 'The sailors were tourists from another country. They didn't know much about Alligator Alley, a monotonous, treacherous road with a high accident rate. 'Alamo,' the lawyers argued, 'were duty bound to ensure the sailors' safe arrival.'

Could it really be that if, on 17 February 1981, I'd fallen asleep at the wheel and caused the accident on that same monotonous, treacherous road, Dollar would have been liable? It seemed to me to be an incredibly over-sensitive and stupid law, but Dade County Court accepted it. More's the pity that the Florida Statute books didn't contain a much more sensible provision to echo what happens in most civilised parts of the world; that a car rental company must offer adequate third-party insurance to their customers.

I subsequently spoke to Brett Panter, one of the two successful lawyers involved in the Ark Royal case, and wished I'd had him on my side. Money would never begin to recompense my loss, but justice and a bursary in my family's name might have eased the pain.

While I looked for a new flying job, I had news that Auntie Frances, my mother's great childhood friend, had died in Edinburgh. Uniquely within my family, I had kept in close contact with her, she had come to our wedding, and she knew Adrienne and the children well. Frances was a good friend to me as well as to my mother, and her whispering, 'Stand firm', in 1981 as I followed the coffins into the funeral service were the perfect words at the most difficult of times.

I got tickets for my father and myself to travel to Edinburgh and booked a hotel for us both. On the morning of the flight my father phoned to say he wasn't coming, because 'It wouldn't do any good.' I went and was pleased to be there.

I returned from Edinburgh to start looking seriously for a job. There was no hurry, because unlike in 1973, I didn't have a family to support or mortgage to pay. But then I suddenly did need a mortgage, because my brother Colin rang to give me the very sad news that he was divorcing his wife Jill. That would mean selling their family home, the house in which I had been welcomed to stay after the accident. I couldn't let that happen, but with two small flats in Barnes, a similar one in France and a much larger flat in Cape Town, I hadn't any spare money. So, I took out a mortgage in Cape Town, so that Colin could keep his house and buy himself an MGB car, like the one I used to have and that he always admired. It was good to do something for him, after his help throughout my life, but especially in the months and years after the accident. He was always at pains to say that he'd written it into his will to repay me, and of course he kept to his word exactly.

It seemed there were many pilots needed for long-haul freight-flying, jobs which offered lots of money, and just a few wanted for short-haul passenger flights, which I'd done enough of already. A good compromise came from Howard Plant, a friend I'd flown with on the Viscount in Scotland. He was now flying Boeing 767's out of Malpensa Airport in Milan and enthused about the airline and the long-haul flying.

I already had a licence to fly the 767 and I'd hardly been to Italy, so Air Europa promised to be an easy and interesting way to continue flying. After a short interview in London arranged by Howard, I joined the airline and then updated my 767 licence, which required three sessions on the British Airways simulator at Heathrow. The sessions began at 2 am on consecutive mornings, probably because the simulator was fully booked during the day. The odd time didn't matter too much because my flat in Barnes was not far away, and I was already so familiar with the 767 that I could (almost) fly it with my eyes half-open.

The Air Europa headquarters was in the town of Gallarate, not far from the newly modernised and extended Malpensa Airport. Billboards everywhere said, 'Malpensa 2000', and there was excitement in the air, as they came towards the end of a massive EU-funded project. This was a brand-new millennium airport, with lots of glass and walkways, and obvious Italian style. There was the same optimism in the Air Europa headquarters at Gallarate. I knew I'd joined a very happy and enthusiastic airline.

After meeting everyone, it was back to the airport, and I was proudly shown one of their almost new Boeing 767/300 planes, which were an extended range version of the ones I'd flown before. Their destinations were mostly new to me, the first four mentioned, Cuba, the Seychelles, Mauritius, and Japan were mouth-watering. That extra range was needed because the flights were long and bordering on the limit for a two-pilot plane, usually starting with a 'short hop' to another city in Italy.

I joined at the same time as Gerald, an ex-Austrian Air Force pilot who had given up flying fast jets and hopped over the border to escape his ex-wife. We instantly got on well, and decided to share a rented flat, somewhere, 'on the lake', and not too far from the airport.

We began our search alongside Lake Maggiore, stopping just to admire the scenery and ask about flats to rent. Right at the end of the lake was Stresa, one of the most beautiful little towns I have seen, a place to linger in and definitely the place to rent a flat.

We found the perfect one, with two bedrooms, and essentially, a balcony overlooking the lake towards the Borromean Islands. It seemed like paradise, perhaps the only downside were the church bells ringing loudly and frequently from the old and well-used church next door.

My ears tuned in after a while because they rang to the signature tune from 'The Archers', the everyday BBC radio story of country folk. Gerald couldn't appreciate that, so he had the bedroom furthest from the bells. My new shared flat on the lake seemed perfect for my Mini Moke, so soon after moving in I went back to Mandelieu and drove it the three hundred miles to Stresa.

The Air Europa Boeing 767 had six Italian cabin crew and most of the copilots I flew with were Italian. They were all a delight to fly with, and to spend time with on long stopovers in places like Cuba. Stresa was a lovely place to live, and I could understand why one of the English captains decided to leave England and move there. After one long overnight flight I walked through the town square and bumped into my brother Colin's son and family, who lived in Switzerland. It was quite a drive from where they lived, but Stresa was their favourite place, as it was fast becoming mine.

I only returned to England twice in my first year, and that was for my father's ninetieth birthday and then Colin's seventieth. I hoped that a family get together was being organised back in England for my father, but deep down I guessed it wouldn't happen because, sadly, my remaining three brothers and sister didn't do things like that. I was disappointed but not surprised when I flew in from Milan and drove down to Maidstone, to find my father sitting by himself, the rest of the family having popped in individually during the day.

I decided that Colin's big day would be different. I booked a table for twenty at Adrienne's favourite restaurant in Maidstone. Before leaving, I phoned every one of my family, including Colin's son in Switzerland, and extracted promises that they would be there on the day, no excuses allowed. I got the usual, 'It's easy for you', from my sister, a response I'd long given up responding to. The truth was, sadly, that my father taught them not to reach out to each other, and that approach fostered constant suspicion and feuds. Through Adrienne's family in Sheffield, I saw a different way of doing things.

I had almost three years flying with Air Europa, enjoying the flying and my days off in Stresa. Unusually for me, I often set off very early for work, so I could park my Moke beside the lake and take in the deep blue water, the boats and the islands. On a bright summer's day especially, when framed by the bright bougainvilleas, it really was a sight worth stopping for, and would prime me for even the longest of flights.

It could well have been that happy period in my life which made me receptive to meeting somebody new. On my infrequent visits to the UK I always travelled north, to visit the grave of course but also to check on houses for sale in North Yorkshire.

Part of my visit always involved a day or two with my friend, Les in Boston Spa near Tadcaster. He had just begun renting part of his house to a Dr. Gina and her German shepherd dog Jaimie, and she almost ran over the two of us as she roared away in her 4 x 4. Once a GP, she was now rising rapidly up the ranks of the NHS, working between their headquarters in Leeds and London.

From that near collision a deep relationship began, despite her living in Yorkshire and me in Italy. I returned to England more frequently, specifically to see Gina and accompanied her to conferences, where she would usually make a speech. I spent cold hours watching her exercise her horse, much as I'd often been frozen watching my daughters twenty years before on the cold bank of the Gare Loch.

One of the many good things about Air Europa was that they reserved a seat in the first-class cabin for a guest of the captain. Now I had somebody to sit in that seat, so in my last year with the airline Gina came with me to the Maldives and Mauritius. Though Cape Town unfortunately wasn't one of Air Europa's routes, Gina and I flew there for the Millennium, and the good time we had was evidenced by a photo of the two of us on the front of the Cape Argus newspaper!

With Gina's help I found a house to buy in Normanby, North Yorkshire, where the sheep just about outnumber the people. As with my rented flat in Stresa, High Gables sat next to a very old church. St Andrews dated back to 1150 and had bells that were heard only on a Sunday morning when Margaret Wood, the eighty-seven-year-old bell ringer, could summon up the strength. She was a lifelong fixture in the village, and a church warden following in the footsteps of her brother and father. She had been born in the big stone house she lived in, which was literally falling down around her ears. There were rumours she left the village to join the war effort but was sent back because of the disruption she caused; she was a woman of clear opinions. As the village elder, Margaret was soon next to me on my first visit and gave me a sort of interview which I passed because she liked me and I instantly liked her.

High Gables looked south across a large field, sloping gradually down to the River Seven as it made its way from the Yorkshire Moors to the much larger River Rye. I thought the scene was beautiful, was Yorkshire through and through, and the perfect place to retire to, so I bought it. I looked forward to updating the inside and beautifying the outside of the house, and then everything would be wonderful. I made plans to build a tennis court, which was something I'd always wanted and where later I would host the Normanby Masters Championship, which annoyingly, my friend Les won. This was the house and village for me, so with more than a tinge of regret, I gave notice to Air Europa of my intentions to leave after three very enjoyable years.

Gina left Yorkshire at the same time, to become a regional director of public health based in Cambridge. I helped her to find a house and accompanied her to one of the Cambridge colleges where she had to introduce herself. I was only allowed to sit in the car outside but felt uniquely proud as she walked to face the assembled audience. It was a pride I felt all those years before when my son walked onstage to give a reading. We were getting very close, and that unfortunately triggered the same reaction that had happened before and would again in the future. As much as I tried, my head would not allow me to bond myself tightly to somebody new. I couldn't drop the past, not yet anyway, so our relationship ended, and I would live in High Gables by myself.

I still had to finish my flying in Italy. After twenty-seven years of flying airliners, my very last landing had to be good, and it promised to be as we approached Malpensa from the south. On a beautiful summer's afternoon, the wind was calm and I enjoyed for the last time that magnificent backdrop of the Alps. It was an important day, as I explained to the passengers. I added that this very last landing was to be as smooth as silk, and for emphasis (after about an hour's instruction from a stewardess), I repeated in Italian, *'Liscio come l'olio'*. I hoped that meant the same thing, but I hadn't got a clue. Confidence was high though, until I selected the first stage of flap for landing; one side went down but the other side didn't, a problem so unusual I hadn't seen it before.

We circled for fifteen minutes while we scanned checklists to come up with the answer; so long that I wondered if some of the passengers thought I had already carried out my 'liscio' landing. Eventually the moment came, and my very last landing was not all that I had hoped for, nor my grasp of Italian sufficient to explain the reason why. It did, however, bring an end to a very pleasant chapter in my life, and I was now ready for North Yorkshire.

The minute I and my furniture lorry arrived at High Gables my new neighbour Margaret was there, and I think by the end of the day most of the one hundred and twenty inhabitants of Normanby had paused outside the gate to catch a glimpse of what was going on.

St Andrews Church and the Rising Sun dominated all. Margaret was a leading light in the first, and during the first few weeks I spent a lot of time in the second. Margaret rang the new bells she had bought for the church, and now promised an extra few pulls on the rope if she saw me coming along the church path. I did that often because I liked the little old church as much as little old Margaret, her 'ask for nothing' values and old-fashioned Yorkshire genuineness appealed to me and as she grew older and increasingly frail, I watched over her.

Most of my belongings had been in store for years, and even in Normanby many boxes remained in the loft unopened. One thing I did notice for the first time was a brown paper parcel, covered in dust and postmarked 'Miami'. Because of that word, I put it to one side until a bright, sunny day. Eventually I was ready and peeled back one corner, enough to see, 'Baptist Hospital, Miami' and my son's name underneath. Here were medical details that I definitely didn't want to see, so I resealed the parcel and put it at the back of a wardrobe. It stayed there until I moved again.

I was a fully retired free man, with lots of time to do everything. That dovetailed nicely with a village like Normanby, where nothing had been done quickly for years. I focused on improving my new house, adding a porch and an oak door before spending weeks painting and tiling the four bathrooms. In my first summer, I planted scores of trees, and hired a mini excavator to make a winding path across the field and down to the river.

In a wooden caravan next to the pub lived Nelson, the village character, who could neither read nor write and was looked on suspiciously by Margaret after trying to steal a sprig of her holly. If he wasn't tending his sheep or stealing holly, Nelson was in the Rising Sun, and over a pint he persuaded me to keep his motley flock of sheep in my field; they all looked rough, but then, so did Nelson.

I was back at last in Yorkshire, proper Yorkshire, and life was good. I walked on the Moors, captivated by the vastness as well as the peace. The skies above were empty, and I began to think of buying a small plane, a simple one, just big enough for me and one other. Not far away, in the village of Wombleton, was an old disused wartime airfield. The control tower and runways were still there but in a sad state. Tucked away in the only usable part of the control tower was Brian, who pointed out on the far side of what was once a massive airfield, a usable hangar where I could keep a plane. I wandered over there and spoke to grey-haired, and long retired Clive, just getting into his French 'Robin' plane. Today he had his long-eared spaniel Dave in the right-hand seat as navigator. Sometimes his wife had the job, but according to Clive it made little difference, except that Dave was, he told me, more sociable.

Wombleton was the airfield for me, and I started looking seriously for a very basic plane. Soon I found one for sale at Old Sarum Airfield near Salisbury. Called a Streak Shadow, it had a lawnmower two-stroke-engine to push along two people sitting one behind the other. Easily taken apart to be towed on a trailer, it seemed just what I was looking for, and I fixed a tow bar to my old Honda.

Colin met me at Old Sarum Airfield, and the plane was waiting, damask red, with cream wheels. It looked great and was ready for me to fly. Ten minutes was enough to convince me to buy it, but I landed and flew another ten minutes with Colin in the back just to make sure. I was shown how to take it to bits, and put on the trailer, and then set off from Wombleton with the trailer and the plane in tow and Colin further back in his car, making sure that nothing fell off.

The airfield was dark and eerie when we arrived, but my new key to the hanger worked and we moved the trailer in. By mid-morning the next day my Shadow was re-built, a mixture of petrol and oil added, and we were ready to fly.

Wombleton was certainly not Heathrow, and only a small part of a taxiway was suitable for take-offs and landings, the massive main runway built hurriedly in 1943 now cratered like the surface of the moon. But unlike most wartime airfields further south, Wombleton was too isolated to be within reach of developers, the old control tower still usable as an office, while ivy clad Nissen huts disintegrated slowly amongst the trees. A magical place for me, and perfect for a first flight in my new plane; with its lawn mower engine, wooden propeller and control column taken from an old Swift post-war fighter.

I was soon airborne, with the plane flying slowly but beautifully, and me enjoying every second of what I was doing and where I was. My next flight had Colin crammed into the back seat, but this time I stayed airborne longer, appreciating for the second time that North Yorkshire was as quiet and peaceful in the air as it was on the ground. With little controlled airspace, we could fly where we wanted, eastwards to the coast at Scarborough, then back over the Moors, and just before landing, a few circles above my neighbours in Normanby.

As we got out of the plane, which was a bit of a struggle, especially for Colin in the back seat, we noticed that my Shadow was exactly the colour of the Cooper 500 racing car, which our next-door neighbour George Wicken raced at Brands Hatch when we were growing up in Maidstone. Damask red with cream wheels.

George had been as fast on his feet as in his Cooper; we once saw him chased by his engineer, jack in hand, for getting too close to his wife. His racing car had looked perfect, with *C'est si bon*, written across the front, so I decided to add those words across the nose of my plane. Word went around Normanby, and within a week, my plane was christened *C'est si bon*, the words neatly inscribed by a farmer's wife sitting alongside the plane on an upturned milk bucket. Perhaps that instilled a bit of George in her, because not long after, I heard she'd run off with another farmer in the village.

Flying my Shadow in the empty skies of North Yorkshire was always fun, but living and flying in Yorkshire was even better when Colin came to visit. We had one memorable summer week together, with lots of flying and a day at the York Races. On a high, we thought we would end the week with a flight in short hops down the east coast to Maidstone.

It was already a hot summer's morning when we set off, me in the front with maps spread over my knees and Colin squashed in the back. We slowly climbed to 2,000 feet and had just crossed the River Humber heading south when the engine stopped. It wouldn't restart, and I didn't have much time to keep trying.

I looked down and saw pylons, with the river just behind. The plane could glide very well, and looking further to my left, I saw a big bright yellow wheat field. Colin seemed unperturbed and pointed out another field, but I'd made up my

212

mind. We landed slowly and safely up a very slight hill and came to a short but not too abrupt stop. We got out to see no apparent damage, and started walking, towards a tractor in the far distance.

The driver was fast asleep and jumped when we tapped on his window. He wasn't at all fazed by our story, as if it happened every day, and said he would take us on his tractor to the farmhouse. The farm owner was just as laid-back, didn't seem bothered about his wheat, and even invited us to his family barbeque he was about to light. Diversions with British Airways were never like that, and we accepted his offer while I got on the phone to my friend Les, who would come and pick us up. After a very nice lunch we left the farm, promising the farmer that we would be back next morning with the trailer to collect the plane.

Next day, Colin wasn't feeling well, but as I set off to collect the plane, he said he felt fit enough to drive home. I was relieved to hear later that he got home safely. Meanwhile the farmer helped me dismantle my plane and load it on to the trailer, obviously pleased to see the wheat stand vertically after the plane was lifted off. There was no sign of damage to his field or my plane, and after thanking him for his hospitality, I towed my Shadow back to where we had started so optimistically the day before, thinking that a lawn mower engine wasn't suitable for a trek down south, however many 'short hops' we split the journey into.

It seemed like a happy ending, and it was until two days later in the early morning when a phone call brought the worst of all news. Colin my brother and very closest of friends, had died of a heart attack. It was the very last thing I wanted or expected to hear, and I was shattered. As I grew up in a family over dominated by my father and consumed with feuds and jealousies, Colin had always been my big supporter and helper.

One of my very earliest memories was of coming home from primary school in tears because my teacher had said I couldn't speak properly. In an instant Colin was on his motorbike, off to give that teacher a piece of his mind. When I was in the cadet force at grammar school, it was Colin who helped me sort the belts and gaiters of my uniform, clean my boots and pack my bag for the annual summer camp.

Whatever achievements I made, from passing the eleven plus, to going solo in my first plane to flying Concorde, it was only Colin who would acknowledge them, always with a 'Very proud of you Alan', on a card or on the phone. That meant a lot, but most importantly for me, in my very darkest times he was always by my side, the one I relied on. At the mortuary and throughout the funeral he had been next to me, he'd let me stay at his house for a year after the accident and stayed up night after night trying to calm me down while I paced his kitchen floor.

In recent years we had been together in Yorkshire, Italy, South Africa, Switzerland and the USA, and never once had a cross word. I suspect it was because he didn't want to put his problems on to me that I was never told of his minor heart attack just a couple of years before. His loss was the biggest of blows, and I prepared to drive down to Maidstone.

I was asked by his daughter Diane to give the eulogy. As much as I hated public speaking it was something that I wanted to do, and to ensure it was right, I practiced on the stairs of Roni Page's house when I called in on the way down from

Yorkshire. As well as being a very dear friend, she was the perfect speaking coach, having had leading roles as a singer and actor in the West End. Speaking from the top of those stairs was exactly how my son Nigel had rehearsed his speech years before. Now it was *like son like father.*

Speaking of Colin came relatively easily in that Barming church, with almost the same congregation as during many recent times. As I finished and looked down at the two separate sides of the congregation, it was poignant to see the usual family factions at a family funeral. Bernard had recently fallen out with my father, so his family kept separate and to one side.

As we came out of the church my eyes fixed on my eldest brother, John. He looked thin and pale and told me that his prostate cancer, which had been under control for years, had suddenly spread. I drove back to Yorkshire hoping that things weren't as bad as he thought, but just two months later he died.

I had lots of lovely memories of John, the eldest in our family of six. Especially I suppose, those rides on the crossbar of his bike, through the North Pole woods to RAF West Malling; they really did kindle my interest in flying. I owed him much more besides. He and Colin were always my staunchest allies in the family, and in two months they were both gone.

It was a well-worn, miserable drive down from North Yorkshire to join the congregation at St Margaret's Church. I looked at my father and wondered what his thoughts were about losing two sons in quick succession.

The service seemed brief and little was said afterwards, possibly because we had all passed that way just a couple of months earlier. It was always a relief to get back to North Yorkshire, but this time, especially so. Tranquillity was timeless; all sorts of things seemed to be happening down south, but thankfully Normanby stayed the same.

The little church played its part, and I didn't need much persuading from Margaret to go to the service the following Sunday. I appreciated even more those extra pulls on the bell rope as I walked down the church path and Margaret's happy smile as I walked through the door. It crossed my mind that the bell rings would be even more uplifting for tiny Margaret, if she didn't let go of the ropes.

On sitting down, it was my normal ritual to say the Lord's Prayer quietly to myself; then to say their names and think of them, each in turn. Inevitably my spirits rose when I looked to that tiny corner below the pulpit, dubbed 'Alan's corner' by Margaret and now bedecked with flowers she had chosen from my garden. The hymns echoed loudly around that tiny ancient church, and I always felt better as I walked out than when I walked in.

I felt settled in North Yorkshire, and for a while anyway, couldn't think of any reason to go anywhere a long distance from home. Getting to Heathrow from Normanby was a trek in itself, so in another spasm of quick decisions, I arranged to sell my flat and boat in France and agreed a three-year rental of my flat in South Africa.

The tenant in Cape Town was to be the American Embassy and their rule was that all tenancies had to be furnished from a central warehouse somewhere in Africa. That meant a return to Cape Town, to empty my four bedroomed flat. After four days of solid packing I was ready for the removers just as they rang the doorbell. As I stood up the telephone rang, and I was given the news that my father had died. I had no choice but to continue moving everything into store, but that evening I caught the flight back to London.

The Atkinson family was dwindling away fast, and for the third time in five months we gathered at the church in Barming. It was December and it was cold, and perhaps that made the service even more dispiriting than the previous one.

My spirits weren't raised when my sister Pauline beckoned me to wind down the car window as I left to drive back to Yorkshire. 'Dad's left his money to me', were her words that rang in my ears as I drove north, a message as surprising as the time and place she'd chosen to give it.

My father's words on his will, 'Distribute as you think fit', were taken exactly as written, though probably not as he had intended. After attempting briefly, for my remaining brother Bernard's sake, to get her to change her mind (I'd already made it clear that anything left to me would be put back in the pot), I gave up.

Just as in Miami fifteen years before, my sanity came first, and I couldn't face a severe family feud on top of everything else. My brother hasn't spoken to his sister since, so prolonging that tradition of family feuds that I had grown up with, moved away from, and certainly could have done without.

22

North Yorkshire seemed the solution to everything, even the ever-lingering frustrations of Miami and the traumas of three more visits to the churchyard at Barming.

By the spring of 2004, I was at relative peace with the world, and in the frame of mind to meet Päivi, a divorced consultant paediatrician from Finland. Now living and working in London, I thought she was both gorgeous to look at and listen to, with her distinctive beautiful accent and an inbred naivety from growing up in the forests of northern Finland. Her family of two lovely daughters and a son was almost a grown-up replica of my family, which immediately flagged up psychological plusses and minuses in my head.

All three were instantly likeable, they were older so direct comparisons couldn't be made, but only time would tell if I could allow them to compete with Nigel, Anna and Lucy in my head. For the moment they were scattered, Anika, the eldest, working for the EU in Brussels, Laura was in London and Henri was still in Helsinki and not yet tempted to head west. In a nutshell, I had met a perfect family that matched my own; if only I'd searched for some good trauma counselling, but it didn't cross my mind.

Päivi combined a delightful mixture of femininity, adventurousness and independence, the last two ingrained from growing up where she did and then battling to become a doctor after divorcing with three young children. Her, 'Let's do it', was a good antidote to my often too careful approach, and before long we were driving around the perimeter of Scotland because, as Päivi said, 'we need to see it'.

A big first step for me was to take her to Helensburgh and introduce her to people that had only ever known me with Adrienne. I even showed her Firlands, the house we had lived in and though I had deep feelings of guilt and disloyalty, Päivi's inbuilt warmth carried the day. Her visit to Helensburgh and into my past led us to take big steps in our lives. Päivi sold her flat in London and moved into High Gables, the first person I had lived with as a partner since Adrienne twenty-two years before. That brought stability as well as tidiness to my life, because being a couple seemed especially essential in a small village like Normanby.

Päivi's want of unspoilt countryside and distant horizons made her fall in love with North Yorkshire, and coming from Finland made her an instant source of wonderment in the village. She had the clear focus that Finns are famous for, and a spiritual side that needed quiet times in the empty church next door, sitting in silence and deep thought. When the Vicar asked her to read one of ten lessons at the carol service, she took it as an honour for Finland as well as herself and read beautifully with tears in her eyes.

Eventually she returned to work as a locum doctor, and I accompanied her to medical conferences around Europe, feeling important with a special tag around my neck as I toured with the rest of the 'doctor's wives' while she was at meetings.

Her parents lived in a house with five saunas next to a massive lake that could be walked over during most of the winter, when the days were misty and gloomy but the nights magical. They spoke little English but her mother would act out what she meant, and I'd give a thumbs-up when I understood. I reminded her father of his best friend growing up during the war, and that made him smile thoughtfully, because those times held bitter memories. The Finns I met were proud patriots, and deeply *'shuspichious'* of their neighbours to the East. They learnt Swedish at school but just 'I surrender' in Russian.

War anniversaries were frequent and well-attended in Helsinki and Päivi and I watched a parade of old soldiers, braving intense cold in grey military greatcoats and fur hats. When it was over Päivi sidled up to a big square-faced and battle-hardened old officer, still standing tall and with medals dripping from his chest. She whispered something, and I saw tears roll down his face.

I asked what she had said. It was, 'Thank you for saving us.'

I was becoming an expert on funerals, and her father's funeral in the forests of Northern Finland stands out for its beautiful simplicity and thoughtfulness. A typically cold and gloomy day was lit by candles in the snow, leading to the burial site deep in the forest. The service began inside a tiny church, where flowers were individually offered to the coffin with short spoken anecdotes told about her father's life. It was moving and impressive in a quiet way, and in stark contrast to the hurried 'by numbers' funerals I had been to recently.

Over many months I'd bored people talking about my refurbished kitchen, so when it was finally finished I planned a 'kitchen-opening' party. I wasn't sure how, but I'd collected the business card of a lady who impersonated the Queen on television and thought she would be ideal to cut the ribbon for my revamped kitchen. I didn't think I'd spoken to her before, so was surprised and delighted when she agreed to come, and I booked her in to a hotel in Malton.

Pretentiousness doesn't go down well in North Yorkshire, and my southern accent meant I was already skating on thin ice. I knew eyebrows would be raised by my notice on the village notice board; 'Royal Appointment at High Gables, Normanby Saturday at 7.30pm'.

Päivi's son Henri flew over from Finland and helped me lay a borrowed red carpet from the front door to the front gate. I set up loudspeakers ready to blast out the Band of the Royal Marines playing the national anthem, and by 7.30 on the day my neighbours were either in my house or peering through the hedge.

Päivi and her lovely daughters, all dressed up for the occasion, joined me on the front porch. At the two-minute warning from the Queen's taxi driver I started the national anthem and she stepped on to the red carpet looking perfect, resplendent in gown, sash, crown and with handbag. As she came through the front door, Margaret leapt to attention at a pace belying her ninety-one years.

In the early hours of the morning I drove a slightly tipsy Queen back to Malton, to find that the front door of her hotel was locked. In the rain we walked round to the sash window of her downstairs room, and I lifted her through, still in her gown, sash and crown. That would have made an even better photo than the one that somehow found its way into a national newspaper, showing the Queen and I sitting round our breakfast table with the caption, 'Yorkshireman has coffee with the Queen'. My daughters especially would have loved to see the Queen sitting at the table where we had so many family, round-table conferences.

Due to the deteriorating condition of her house Margaret now lived in just three downstairs rooms because it was too dangerous to go upstairs. Heating was intermittent and she spent cold days wearing her big heavy coat. But she was happy being next to the church, and in the village where she had spent her life. Now she needed somewhere safe and warm to live and I was surprised and delighted when she was persuaded to look at houses for sale.

We found the ideal bungalow in Kirkbymoorside, just two miles away, next to another church and opposite her doctor's surgery. Even though I offered dinner for every night she stayed there, and she liked the property and bought it, she wouldn't live in it. After one night there, next morning at 8.30 sharp, she was standing on the pavement with her small suitcase ready to 'go home.' Her heart was in Normanby, so eventually after a conference with her goddaughter in Harrogate, her new bungalow was rented and I helped her buy a large caravan which sat next to her beloved St Andrews.

I fancied one last trip to the USA, anywhere but Florida, and ideally with spaces and mountains bigger than in North Yorkshire. Somebody suggested a house exchange, and through the internet I arranged to swop houses for six weeks with one in Durango, South Colorado. An American professor and his wife were happy to live in sleepy North Yorkshire while we lived in their much bigger timbered house 7000ft up in the mountains of Falls Creek. It was one of a hundred large houses, all with an acre of forest where animals including bears roamed at will. At the same time, we would also swop cars, because I was wary of renting a car in the USA.

We enjoyed those six weeks so much that we decided we should live there, and fortuitously, it seemed, the building plot with the best view of all was now vacant, a fire having recently burnt down the house that had been there. My enthusiasm to move west lasted about three days, because of what seemed like the insurmountable hurdle of getting a green card to live in the USA. Päivi's enthusiasm was forever. She said, 'We will find a way'.

While Päivi schemed and planned for lofty things, I opted for the pathetic alternative of extending my house to give better views, though they could never match those from 7000ft in Falls Creek. We had ideas that were 5000 miles apart, but in most ways, we were getting very close, and inevitably for me, that brought on my usual panic and sadly the end of our relationship. We had become fully integrated in my beloved North Yorkshire, and I was very fond of her family, imagining her elder daughter, the older daughter that I would have loved to have. One or two of my closest friends said what I knew to be true; I'd found at the eleventh hour a way forward. That, suddenly, was the problem. I became ultra-sensitive about my own family, crticising Päivi for not mentioning my family more often, or for forgetting one of my big days. It was all trivial, except to me at that time, but the pressure built up until I reached a tipping point.

Päivi *did* find a way, she swiftly got her green card, married an American doctor she met while white-water rafting on the Colorado River, and now divides her time between Phoenix and a brand-new house built on the plot we had both seen in Falls Creek. There's a lesson there somewhere about fortune and the brave.

Ending things with Päivi, I knew was a spectacular own goal, and yet I couldn't stop it happening. I needed to get away and think about things, so next day I flew to my flat in Cape Town which was now empty. The long flight gave me time to do that thinking about everything that had just happened and kept happening. Pointedly I suppose, a friend had recently reminded me that the definition of insanity was doing the same thing over and over and expecting a different result. I wasn't sure whether I was expecting a different result, but I needed help and at last I knew it. Once in Cape Town I was given the name of Bill Petrie, a trauma counsellor, and I booked ten sessions.

Bill lived in a remote spot overlooking Hout Bay, on the green and wetter side of Table Mountain. Our hour-long sessions were in a small wooden shack, a short woodland pathway from the house, surely the quiet natural detached spot in which I could unwrap my inner self.

I sat opposite Bill, and immediately his black beard and piercing brown eyes made me think of Jack the Ripper, and if I hadn't been transfixed by those eyes I might have rehearsed some karate moves. Then we started, with me apprehensive and unbelieving, and Bill having seen it all before.

He was brilliant. His sharp eyes focused my mind and extracted the absolute truth, however much it hurt. That was his skill; not long before, he had been invited to London to help in the aftermath of the Paddington rail disaster.

His first question was the obvious one, but seldom asked since I met the Miami police the day after the accident, 'What happened?'

I told him, exactly as I remembered from that night in Miami. He wanted more, with all the detail, and that hurt,

224

but my pauses didn't matter, because Bill sat patiently, probing.

That detail, and actually putting it in to words, sort of cleansed me and settled some demons; it established the facts and eradicated the more horrific imaginings. He led me to places I was frightened to touch, asking questions and waiting expectantly in silence until the full memory came out.

Beginning with that first question came the various strands, session by session. Why did I have my boxes? What was I hiding away? How bad did I think it would be if my heart was on my sleeve, rather than in that box?

The questions went on and on, and many times were difficult, but Bill's methods combined with the isolation of the setting drew forth fears that were better out than in. Perhaps I needed to face up to the past in order to live with it.

I mentioned the pressures I felt four times a year as my 'big dates' loomed up. He asked, 'What do they want from you?'

My answer, painstakingly drawn out, was, 'To think of them but to get on with a happy and successful life.' Bill expanded that, saying they would want me to let go, just a bit, and that, 'they would understand.'

Each of those ten sessions built on the one before, all giving me greater perspective over what had happened. I left feeling freer and calmer about everything, and those 'big dates', though still big, became more manageable. At last I appreciated the skill of a good trauma counsellor, and wished I had taken the counselling step much earlier, though I still had that fear of disturbing a hornet's nest. I think we agreed that there is no cure for grief, but good counselling had a place to play in tinkering with the pressure valve. Those ten sessions did exactly that and I returned to Yorkshire feeling much calmer, if not cured.

While Päivi doctored and skied and lived the high life in the USA, I shuffled around the little-changing world of North Yorkshire. I sold my temperamental Shadow plane with its lawnmower engine, and started looking for a reliable and more modern replacement.

Friedrichshaven Airfield on the shores of Lake Constance in Germany still had the enormous old hangers that used to house Zeppelin airships. Now it was home to an annual light aircraft exhibition, showing just about every type available to buy. My eyes focused on one made in Germany, a two seat, carbon fibre plane called a Remos GX, and after three days of deliberation and a quick test flight I ordered one. Two months later it was ready, and I flew it back from the factory at Peenemunde, to the east of Berlin. The last leg of a long flight took me to over-head Sherburn Airfield in Yorkshire, and I made a last-minute decision to land there, for one of the airfield café's famed bacon sandwiches as well as to show the plane to my friend Les who flew from there.

I spent longer there than intended, and left Sherburn on a perfect summer's evening, in carefree mood even before I saw my part of North Yorkshire stretched out in front of me. It was quiet, with no other planes around, so I turned off the navigation screen and instead followed the country lanes I knew like the back of my hand.

York was first to my left, then the white dome of Castle Howard, followed by the big wheel at the fairground near Pickering, till after forty minutes I could see the massive but now broken, wartime runways of Wombleton.

The light was fading fast as I landed, and I hadn't heard a word the whole flight. Everything was dead still and pitch black as I pushed my new plane in to the hanger after sitting in the cockpit for probably an hour, enjoying my new toy and thinking to myself, not for the first time, *this is my part of the world*.

That silent flight sticks in my mind, more than any reheated take-off on Concorde, because it was just me, in my own plane and in North Yorkshire. I felt settled again, helped I'm sure by the new plane and the counselling in Cape Town.

In every one of my seven Novembers in Normanby I'd seen Margaret trudging around the houses and farms selling Remembrance Day poppies, whatever the weather. On one particularly wet day I drove her from farm to farm, and found out it was her seventieth year of poppy-selling, without ever even a glimmer of recognition. I wrote to the British Legion who agreed that seventy years was special, so they suggested a party at my house, for which they would provide a cake, champagne and a box full of poppies, as well as tell the local newspaper.

Margaret's friends and neighbours were all there, and next morning the front page of the *Ryedale Gazette and Herald* showed Margaret happy and proud, sitting under a cloud of falling poppies. More was to come, because I was asked by the man from the British Legion if Margaret and I would be interested in going to the next Buckingham Palace garden party. And of course, we were.

The official invitation from the Palace made Margaret's year if not her life, and on the big day we caught the train down to London and had tea in the RAF Club before walking across St James's Park to the Palace. Margaret was in heaven; tiny and frail as she was, she wrestled her way to the front of the line-up to be closest to Prince Charles as he walked past. Wearing her brother's wartime medals gleaming proudly on her chest.

For a while I was engrossed in North Yorkshire and flying my plane. On a particularly calm day, I gave Margaret her very first flight, at the age of ninety-four, so she could see from the air everything she had known for so long on the ground.

I'd almost forgotten about Cape Town, till I heard that there was talk of a gigantic football stadium being built on the golf course next to my flat for the 2010 World Cup. I flew down, to be assured by the owner of the Metropolitan Golf Club that they had a lease until 2009 and so 'there was no way a football stadium could be built on the course.' Good news, but just to convince myself, I joined the crowd at organised meetings, where everybody seemed passionately certain that it could never happen. A female solicitor chaired the meetings and she gave chapter and verse of the long planning process for that location, so a 2010 deadline would never be met. She said that the golf course site was voted last of the six considered locations, mainly due to the traffic problem in getting people there. Apparently though there were threats that if the stadium wasn't built on that golf course, houses would be, once the lease ran out. That was for another day, and I flew back to London convinced that the golf course and my Table Mountain views were safe.

Two months later. in March 2007, I got a call to say that the building of the stadium on the golf course was about to start. I was told that FIFA, the International Federation of Association Football had insisted on having the backdrop of Table Mountain for the new stadium, dismissing all the real negative arguments against the size and location. Arguments that never went away after the stadium was opened and it became an expensive white elephant. It reminded me of my battle to obtain a prosecution in Miami; whatever the right or wrong, or in this case the democratic vote, nobody really listens unless you have an expensive lawyer or a baying media behind you.

My flat in Cape Town was ten floors up, so it was high enough to look over the new stadium. But the thought of living there while the work was going on, being next to a noisy stadium instead of a quiet golf course, and seeing at close quarters how decisions were made in Cape Town, made me decide to sell.

Change once again was in the air, and I started to think about moving from North Yorkshire, something I thought I would never do. Curiously I made the decision during the harvest festival service, in the church next door. It was always the nicest of all village occasions, and Margaret had given me the usual big smile and that extra pull on the bells as I walked in. Farmers and their families filled the front pews, and baskets of wheat, wools and various breads were spread out in front of the alter. For weeks I'd watched the combine harvesters on the far side of the river working under headlights when it got dark. It was all very emotive, though it was a couple of verses from 'We Plough the Fields and Scatter' and the tea and cakes afterwards that I looked forward to most.

I definitely wasn't one of them, but the farmers had welcomed me to the village, and we'd talked across the river or in the pub. But now suddenly, in that best of all church rituals, it hit me that the village of Normanby belonged to them and I was really a square peg in a round hole. I don't know if it was the sale of my last outpost in Cape Town, or if village life wasn't the same without Päivi, or it was just my recurring restlessness, but in that one gloomy moment I decided I was a southerner who couldn't live long enough to really belong amongst the North Yorkshire farmers. And like all my whims over the last thirty years, my mind was made up and I was on a mission to move. I would return to the sunny uplands of the south before life completely passed me by.

It's a pity my house sold so quickly because another spring in Normanby might have made me change my mind. As might a revisit to that definition of insanity, because I was repeating what I'd done so many times before. But now it was too late, and once again everything would go in to store, the difference this time being that I had no plan of what to do next.

I decided to rent in Salisbury and would have gone there except at the very last minute the American owner of the property decided they wanted to live in it. My friend Christine had a small house to rent, so for no particular reason I spent the next four years in East Grinstead, East Sussex.

The new owner of High Gables enthusiastically got on with making the changes I had planned to do, giving *him* those wonderful views of the river and fields. Nelson's fifty rough sheep were replaced by six designer ones, all, I was told, with degrees from Nottingham University. They had that look about them when I came to visit Margaret next door a few weeks later.

For the first time in forty years, I didn't own a house. More importantly, I'd thrown away the tranquility of Normanby and the love and stability that had come with my relationship with Päivi. My inner compass rocked wildly, and I clutched at fanciful straws, having an offer accepted on a house in Claremont, Cape Town. Perhaps it was as well that a tearful call from the South African estate agent ended that plan, telling me there had been a mistake and the house had been sold to somebody else.

I moved my plane to Deanland Airfield near Lewes, where I discovered that the owner also had a Remos GX, one of only five in the UK. For a year or two I spent my time flying, looking in estate agent's windows, and traipsing round houses for sale. That was until I met Nicky from South Africa, a blonde and beautiful expert on interior design who I was introduced to in Cape Town.

Nicky was a capable all-action woman who had just come down from Johannesburg after putting together the Decorex SA exhibition and a TV series called *Design Inspiration*. As if that wasn't enough, she had finished two books on first the houses and then the gardens of South Africa, and was now living between Cape Town and France. Long divorced, with two delightful grown up sons, I couldn't understand how she had time for a homeless man from the UK, but she made time and even invited me on a tour of some of the homes and gardens she'd just written about. It was our shared sense of humour that propelled our relationship relentlessly onwards and upwards until, after two very happy years, we had a lavish engagement party under the Cape Town sun.

It was a giant step for both of us and pulled depths of emotion from me that only the accident had previously brought out. I was just one short step from a lovely new wife and family, but the situation rang a giant alarm bell, because I'd been this way before.

I loved Nicky and hoped against hope that the thirty years since the accident would allow me to surrender the past. Nicky told me that one of my friends had advised her to move quickly with a wedding date, 'or it might not happen at all', and hearing that actually brought all the arguments in my head right to the fore. I felt it and Nicky felt it, because just after I'd tried to phone Bill Petrie for some counselling, Nicky told me that she had arranged three sessions with a local vicar, who was a part-time therapist.

I chose the soft option of the vicar, for the same old reason that things were going well and I didn't want to disturb a hornets' nest. Those sessions *were* gentle, we skirted around generalities without Bill's rapier incisiveness, so I finished the third session happy that nothing had been disturbed and literally trusting to God that I could carry things through.

The following summer went well; we spent time in England and flew my plane. On 13 October I went to the grave, for Nigel's birthday, as I always did, but this time with Nicky. My family was once more centre-stage and with that came the misgivings about what I was doing. Once again, I became very sensitive about my family, looking for sleights against them when none were intended. In hindsight it was trivial and undeserved, but I was on a path I couldn't escape from, and back in Cape Town I ended our relationship. I threw away the chance of a loving replacement family, because my head wouldn't let me do it.

Looking for a house in East Grinstead seemed very lonely and mundane after my recent travels with Nicky to Zimbabwe, Natal, Cape Town, and Provence. I felt exhausted by just speaking to an estate agent, so one day I short-circuited the whole procedure and decided on Dorset, a county I didn't know except that it was smaller, warmer and perhaps more mani-cured than Yorkshire.

My search had got narrower, and perhaps it was divine

inspiration that led me, on a canal boat with my RAF friend Robin, to read a Saturday *Daily Telegraph,* where my eyes by default always went to the property page. Apparently, you lived longer if you lived in Broadstone, Dorset, though I couldn't see a guarantee. I did see, at the bottom of the page, a picture of a house for sale in that same small town, and it looked a bit different from the thousands I'd seen previously. I drove down to see it and in real life it still looked different and interesting, so after some negotiation and on a whim based on frustration with estate agents, I bought the house.

Anticipating the chaos of all my possessions, from Cape Town, France, East Grinstead and North Yorkshire at last coming under one roof in Dorset, 'simplify' became my watch-word, and I even toyed with selling my plane. Its inordinately complicated yearly service was due, which meant flying it to an airfield north of London and leaving it there, which would complicate my move.

I placed one advert on the internet just to test the response. Marcos from Reichenbach in Switzerland was so keen that he caught the plane to Gatwick on the understanding that he might need a return ticket. After much thought, and Marco's promise that I could return any time to Switzerland to fly the plane, I decided to sell. He sat beside me for the flight to Reichenbach, stopping one night, en-route at Wiesbaden in Germany. The approach to Reichenbach was stunningly beautiful, the airfield in a steep valley, with mountains on three sides and Lake Thun at one end. When I asked about the small crowd I could see, Marco said it was his birthday.

I stopped the plane in front of what seemed like half the village, a brass band and a table full of cake and wine. Amongst them was Andrew, my brother Colin's son, who lived nearby in Berne. After much handshaking, singing, cake for me, and fuel for the plane, there was time for a final flight as owner of G-GXAL with Andrew around the mountains and lakes of that beautiful part of Switzerland. I wondered what Colin would have thought; and it seemed right, not benevolent, to give half my proceeds to Andrew. I was chipping away at my debt to him for his help to me in the darkest of times, and that made me feel relieved rather than good.

I left Reichenbach with a few full stops added to my hurly burly life and certain that Remos G-GXAL would rather be based in Reichenbach than just about anywhere else in the world. And I did return two years later, with Liz, to fly 'my' plane.

At last came the move. My friend Les from Yorkshire came to help me sort the initial chaos and Nicky from Cape Town popped in on a rare trip to London to cheer me up, saying, 'This is the last house you should have bought.' It was in the wrong part of the country perhaps, but I thought the house was attractive and had potential. I'd just have to make changes, as I had done on every house I'd bought. The difference now, was that I was older, and things took longer to improve.

After two years, I'd reached an impasse, but salvation came after I was invited to a retirement party in Sheffield. Following an outstanding university career, Liz had long before left the academic life to take up a position as senior dental partner in a private practice close to the University of Sheffield. Now, many happy and successful years later, she was selling her dental practice and retiring to enjoy new ventures. We had kept in contact, since being neighbours, twenty-five years before, when I tried my short-lived experiment of living in Sheffield and commuting to Heathrow. When I couldn't make one of my important dates in Sheffield, it was Liz who would place some flowers, and coincidentally was dentist to Peter, Adrienne's brother.

I was pleased to be invited to her retirement party just over the border from Sheffield into Derbyshire. Typically, Liz, volunteered to drive down to Dorset and help, initially with the things that had caused the impasse, choosing doors, tiles, paints and fabrics. She would drive down to spend hours in Topps Tiles or Poole Joinery, and as with her visits to the grave in Sheffield, I appreciated not just her help but her selflessness. Working weekends in Dorset, became romantic weekends in Yorkshire, weeks in Spain and eventually months together in Cape Town. We finished the house and sold it, buying one together near the coast in West Sussex. Unlike the house in Dorset, this wasn't in uncharted territory but near friends and places I knew from living in West Chiltington, twenty years before. A home, rather than a staging post.

Fittingly, it was Liz, who finally opened the dusty brown paper parcel with the Miami postmark, which through circumstance and apprehension had laid untouched for years. She looked beyond the first few pages of medical information, which I hadn't wanted to see and saw page after page of legal documents underneath them, telling the story of what my lawyers and advisor did or didn't do in Miami. The facts and the fiction, the doubts and the failings of my long and painful battle for any recognition in the civil courts of Miami, having failed to get even a hint of justice in the criminal courts. The long, sometimes uplifting, but rarely cathartic process of writing my story could begin.

We are now together in a lovely home, rather than a house, as a team rather than separate players. Liz couldn't provide the replacement family I'd striven for, but instead gives the quiet ongoing love, support and stability that gives me peace. Uniquely, of all the women I had become involved with in the years since the accident, only Liz really understood the importance of my memory trail back to Sheffield. And of course, she comes from Sheffield, where my first love story began so optimistically almost fifty years ago.

First ever flight for Margaret, my next-door neighbour
in North Yorkshire at the age of ninety-four

Nigel, forever my hero

Adrienne

Afterword

Dr. Alan Wolfelt, a Director of the Centre for Loss and Life Transition in Colorado, USA, has written many books about grief. He says, *The next time someone asks if or suggests that you're reaching closure, tell them there is no such thing. All we can hope for is to reconcile our grief, integrating our new reality of life without the physical presence of the person who has died.* He also says, *Grief is not a sign of weakness, it's a sign of love.*

If I'm given a random date in the seventies I automatically relate to the birthday of my son in October 1969. A date in the eighties to the accident in 1981. After forty years I still drive to the grave in Sheffield for birthdays and anniversaries. Last December, and in a moment of shock when I fell into my icy pond, I instinctively called out Adrienne, the name of my wife from forty years ago. I plainly didn't find 'closure', so I'm heartened when Dr. Wolfelt says there is no such thing.

Did I achieve his alternative, which was to reconcile my grief and integrate my new reality of life? Well, I did stand firm, but it was often hard going. Twice I had clear signals in my head that I needed to let go. The first time was during the lengthy and intense Concorde conversion course, when I was happy to let the Miami case slip away. The second was many years later, when flying long hours out of Milan with Air Europa I took an almost instant decision to retire and live away from it all in North Yorkshire. Financially, neither were good moves, but they kept me sane.

I'm told that grief makes you mad, and perhaps that's true. Certainly, it reconfigured my life and made me restless, constantly rejecting the life I was leading. I challenged myself by flying Concorde, and I kept myself interested and busy with small planes and a boat and constant moves. I went to exciting places and met interesting people but was never really satisfied. I put that down to what happened in February 1981. Perhaps I was waiting for something too wonderful to come out of something so awful. I stood firm, but I couldn't stand still, and perhaps deep down part of me hasn't fully accepted what happened that night.

Some people thought that I returned to work too quickly. At the time I could think of nothing else to hold on to, so I grasped my job for stability. My job was essential because I had a deep belief that Adrienne and I had put too much into our lives to let it all go.

It was twenty years later when Vitaly Kaloyev, a Russian architect, faced a similar situation. While he waited at Barcelona airport for his wife and two children to arrive from Moscow, their plane collided with a DHL Boeing 757 over Lake Constance in Austria. All the occupants on their UNESCO charter flight for children and all on the 757 were killed. The accident was late at night and blame was put on the Air Traffic Control company in Zurich controlling the flights.

Kaloyev stopped working and spiralled into a pit of depression, suffering a nervous breakdown, refusing to shave and constantly wearing black. He wrote a eulogy which he posted online in tribute to his son; 'Konstantin would have become a good, well-educated person, useful to society, were it not for this tragedy, which I cannot get over. I have no strength.' At the memorial service for the first anniversary of the crash he asked the head of the Air Traffic Control company if he could meet the controller responsible but received no response. Kaloyev sought accountability for the accident and said a personal apology would do. When that was denied, and driven by grief and frustration, he travelled to Switzerland and murdered the man he held responsible, the man he wasn't allowed to meet. He said he did it to 'protect the honour of his children,' and 'if he'd invited me into the house, the conversation would have happened in softer tones and the tragedy might not have happened.'

Murder was obviously wrong and he was given a prison sentence, later reduced, but in Kaloyev's mind the crime brought justice in the only way left open to him, the personal apology having been denied. That extreme action, sad and wrong as it was, brought *him* some sort of closure, because he found direction, married again and had a new family.

I have to say that the inaction in Miami gave me brief thoughts of returning there to confront a certain Mr. Anderson; probably from that same combination of grief and frustration that drove Kaloyev. Those thoughts didn't last, but that silence from Miami made a difference to my life in that the whole tragic event was always open-ended. Four people were killed, yet there was silence. I heard nothing from the Florida police once I left their shores. The lawyers that hovered to take up my case faded away once it became clear that Anderson had no assets and little insurance, leaving the 'money-route' the only way open for any semblance of justice. I started off in the civil court on a case 'we were bound to win', but the selected two lawyers I hired went off at a tangent while the statute of limitations expired.

241

Getting nowhere and not being heard was, as Vitaly Kaloyev found, a big driver towards insanity, and that's why I let events in Miami slip away. But those events were still 'hanging in the air', leaving silence instead of justice without even an acknowledgement that something bad and wrong happened that night. That frustrating silence perhaps didn't drive me mad, but it inevitably affected the rest of my life and left those brief and inadequate words etched on the gravestone in Sheffield as the only tangible marker I have for what happened on the night of 17 February 1981. My innocent and beautiful family deserved far more.

Nevertheless, I coped in my own way and in most ways; probably doing as Dr Wolfelt suggests and integrating a new way of life. My two techniques of 'diversion therapy' and 'putting into boxes' allowed me to switch on and off my big emotional downturns and concentrate on what I had to do. It was pretending, but it kept me flying and estate agents busy as I bought, changed, and sold alongside an expensive and exciting lifestyle that many others eagerly latched on to, hopefully for the right reasons.

Unfortunately, grief had to come out, and hiding it drove away the help and supportive conversations that I needed. I quickly discovered that whereas a divorced wife might be spoken about in hushed tones, a deceased one is hardly spoken about at all, and deceased children are a definite no-go area. Death is a difficult subject to broach anyway, so hiding my grief readily persuaded others that all was under control. Now most people I know assume I am writing a book about flying. Others who do know of the accident might hang on nervously when riding with me at night, thinking that my history of night-driving isn't good. I didn't put anyone right; I kept everything in my head because that way I kept in control.

People found novel ways of reacting to the loss of my family, not for malicious reasons but to help them confront it. A long-time friend from North Yorkshire, for example, has often said that I couldn't have seen much of my family because I was an airline pilot, which in his mind presumably decreases the loss I feel and therefore the embarrassment he feels. The truth was of course the opposite. I was at home so much in Scotland that Adrienne was able to commute for a year to Jordanhill College in Glasgow and qualify to teach children with quite awful disabilities; a time when the children found out that I really was a dreadful cook.

I became a bit of an ego trophy; I was left open-mouthed and speechless at my nephew's wedding when guests were dragged across the dance floor to meet me with the loud introduction 'Here's the man who had that awful accident.' I also frequently heard, 'I don't know how you stand up.'

I established my coping strategies, and surrendered on the legal issues, so life for me once more went generally onwards and upwards. My optimism and sense of humour returned, and with it my life-long desire to get from A to B without the boring bits in between. I owned lots of gadgets and did lots of things, but water-skiing off my little boat in the south of France, or even flying Concorde to Cape Town, was as nothing compared to what I really wanted; not that exciting stuff but a return to a family life, something akin to what I'd had before. Adrienne had always said, 'After wallpapering, being a father is your best talent.'

Perhaps a good counsellor at an early stage would have pointed out the obvious; if you lose something very precious, the answer is to replace it with something similar, however much that hurts and however much you might feel the need to delay. That was my panacea, or as close as I could get. I was young enough to have another family or to be involved with a young family and that was what I was good at. I had many chances of re-kindling a family life, and twice was engaged to lovely women with delightful children. There were my chances, and the engagements wrung tremendous outpourings of emotion from me. But my head wouldn't allow it, and as marriage beckoned I called a halt, causing deep unhappiness to everybody, including myself.

A psychiatrist might say that I fear losing the people or things that I cherish, so I pre-empt that loss at a time of my choosing. It's a trait I definitely have, with possessions anyway. I rushed to sell my boat, my plane, my marina flat in France and my apartment in Cape Town when I was enjoying them most. Not for the proceeds, because some were given away, but as part of the psychological process of wanting a 'permanent good' that couldn't be lost.

But with the women in my life the reason was more profound; a new life with somebody else would wipe the slate clean and leave my precious family behind… something I couldn't let happen. I hadn't come to terms with the loss of my own family, and good, early counselling *might* have helped. What I suspect might have helped even more was lifting the closed curtain that still hid what happened that dark night in Florida. I failed in the justice system of Florida, or more truthfully, that system failed me. Like the Grand Old Duke of York, I marched to the top of the hill, not with ten thousand men but with Adrienne, Nigel, Anna-Jane and Lucy-Claire. We had just reached the top when we were pushed off, by a rusty old car going backwards with the driver holding a drink. So quietly that the authorities didn't seem or want to notice.

I never settled but I ploughed on and I'm grateful that at the eleventh hour I found Liz. Her love and patience, (and her unstinting work helping me write this book), got me looking upwards again. Perhaps 'getting over it' or a return to family life was impossible for me, but I found a Sheffield girl with a heart of gold who makes me happy. Thank you, Liz.

Epilogue

My hope is that this book comes across as a love story, above and beyond the shenanigans that surrounded events in Miami. My family deserves nothing less. I think I've come to terms with the imponderables, and no longer look skywards and ask why things contrived together to place us exactly in the wrong place at the wrong time. I accept begrudgingly that four wonderful young people were killed and lives changed, not through an Act of God, but because somebody with a drink in his hand slammed his old battered car into reverse gear and drove directly in front of us.

What I find hard to accept is the judicial silence that followed, and what I still see as the injustice and inhumanity of it all. Now, with perhaps a slightly less jaundiced eye, I look back from a distance and ask professional experts what should have happened and if anything has changed.

The first surprise is to find that car hire insurance for foreign visitors to the USA, so inadequate in 1981, still *can* be. It so shocked us back then that my relative and 'legal advisor' penned a press release and we both did a fifteen-minute exposé on Breakfast TV. The chairman of ABTA (Association of British Travel Agents) took part, and it seemed to shock him too. I had letters from others who fell foul of a giant loophole in US third-party car insurance; a country where one in seven drivers is completely uninsured - as compared to one in thirty-six in the UK.

In most countries, by law, third-party insurance has to be

unlimited, so a driver and their passengers are fully protected from damage caused by another driver, who legally should have that same cover. If he doesn't, in the UK the Motor Insurance Bureau steps in and acts as that driver's third -party insurance. It's a totally different situation in the USA, where compulsory third-party insurance is minimal and varies from state to state.

In Florida in 1981 it was $20,000, a figure that hasn't changed since. That's perfectly adequate for American drivers, because their own domestic car insurance follows the driver and not the car, and becomes their 'primary cover' when they hire a car. For Europeans and for visitors from most of the rest of the world that's not the position, so they need 'top-up' insurance to be offered by the car rental company or they drive off into the Florida hinterland with inadequate third-party insurance. Despite ticking every box on the car rental form and hearing, 'Buddy, you are fully covered' from the rental agent, that is all I had in 1981.

One definition of a quagmire is 'a soft boggy area of land that gives way underfoot'. A legal quagmire is 'an awkward, complex, or hazardous situation.' I think both definitions applied to the Florida car rental insurance situation I stumbled across in 1981. A situation so perfectly summed up by my legal advisor Alistair on Breakfast TV, 'Would you *knowingly* drive a hire car with your wife and three children, *knowing* that you had no uninsured motorist cover, *knowing* that there was no equivalent of the Motor Insurers' Bureau and *knowing* that other motorists were allowed to drive motor cars with only $20,000 liability insurance?' I could have added that one in five drivers in the state of Florida was completely uninsured at that time.

In his press release, Alistair said 'Every prudent American driver takes out UM (Uninsured Motorist) insurance, usually limited to $1,000,000.' And yet if you rented a car, you weren't even offered it.

It was a hazard without a solution, a wrong to be put right, because something essential was missing from those rental contracts in Florida. Then and now, I thought the negligence lay there, in those contracts, and looking through the legal paperwork, it was a view that seems to have been offered in the advice given to Lawyer S at the time; 'Our course of action would seem to be against the leasing company for failure to acquire the proper amount and kind of insurance.'

His advice was prophetic; 'We will have a tough row to hoe against the insurance company'.

In the event our lawsuits were against the insurance company (changed mid-action) and a bankrupt company, and that certainly proved an impossible row to hoe. It would have been a lot more satisfying to me if our lawsuits had been against Dollar for those inadequate contracts. Perhaps a wrong could then have been put right and appropriate UM insurance offered to everybody.

I asked my school friend John Chrystal, who still lives in Connecticut, and he confirms that he and his wife both have $1,000,000 uninsured motorist coverage which would apply to any car they hired. An American is automatically fully covered to the extent he wants and is willing and able to pay for, but the visitor is not; that was the problem I found in 1981 and recently I wondered if anything was different forty years later.

It *is*, but only for the wary. The loophole we exposed in 1981 was closed by Hertz, who took over Dollar. They started offering a special 'LIS package' *for foreign renters only* five years after my accident. Their vice-president said, 'It clearly makes sense from a protection point of view for foreigners renting a car in the USA to consider the LIS option'. If it made sense in 1986 it made sense in 1981, but the car rental companies in the USA and the UK Association of British Travel Agents looked on and did nothing.

The Hertz LIS package was laudable but was eventually stopped, apparently by the powerful insurance lobby, but thereafter, 'add-ons' to rental car insurance *might* be offered when you hire a car. 'Might' because it depends on where and how you hire a car. As Mark Bower, CEO of Clarify Car Hire said in November 2018, 'It is still a dangerous mess for visitors from Europe to the USA who don't understand the way US car insurance works, or rent from American agents who might not be trained to appreciate the insurance we need.' All of this seems incredible, in a state where one in four drivers is now completely uninsured, but perhaps explained by the reality that cheap insurance sells better than adequate insurance.

Transatlantic communication before the internet was difficult, but of course there were telephones, and the American Embassy existed for urgent and important matters; I went there in 1984 to give an affidavit under oath. So does anything explain or excuse the way the prosecution of Mr. Anderson was handled? No, says Inspector Matt Butler of the Serious Collision Investigation Team for Dorset, Devon and Cornwall who I went to see in December 2018. I showed him the sketchy Accident Report and he said it wasn't too different to the ones they used until recently in the UK. He noted a file reference number, the mention of witnesses and photographs; all indicating to him that a much more comprehensive accident *file* would have existed. The Inspector said I should have known what was in that file and asked to comment on it. He told me,

'As the victim and next of kin I would expect you to be made aware of all the available evidence, so that you understand what happened and are prepared for what might be said at a court case or inquest.'

If I *had* seen it, I would have looked for mention of the can in Anderson's hand and seen whether he had been checked for alcohol after his day fishing. I could have questioned the premise that he was making a U-turn; my clear recollection was of him driving backwards at right angles, just a few feet in front of me.

The secrecy of that accident report file was as unjust in 1981 as it would be now, and Inspector Butler described the lack of communication from the Miami police as both wrong and inhumane. Without actually seeing that file he could only generalise about the offence, but to pull out on to a main road without looking he said would normally be classed as 'careless' in the UK, although the consequence of four deaths might ratchet up the resulting sentence. Further details, that Anderson reversed in front of two sets of full headlights or the contents of that drink in his hand could have elevated the offence to 'causing death by dangerous driving', or the post 2008 UK offence of, 'Causing death by careless or inconsiderate driving'. All those details, incriminating or otherwise, should have been within the full accident report together with my necessary evidence. It was curious, he said, that I was never shown it.

I went to Miami to see the district attorney twice and the state attorney once, and was promised, but never given, evidence of a prosecution. Just recently, I spoke to Ibis Heras, an executive assistant at the Office of the State Attorney in Miami. He couldn't find anything on record about a prosecution of a Robert Anderson at that time. Except, intriguingly, there was a Mr. Robert Anderson who appeared on criminal files one month after my accident for manslaughter, for which he was later given fifteen years in prison. This was probably a red herring, but with absolutely no evidence of a prosecution I look for reasons. Could it be that the Miami authorities abandoned me because Mr. Anderson was facing much more serious charges closer to home? Or is the answer much simpler? Was Mr. Anderson given a community service sentence as I was told on my third visit to Miami? The state attorney had told me in January 1985 that Anderson *would* be prosecuted, and the district attorney in December 1986 said he *had* been prosecuted. If it did happen between those two dates, there was a delay of at least four years. That seems strange and is made more disquieting in that I was never sent an accident report, never asked to give evidence, nor ever informed directly of any outcome, if it happened.

Bearing in mind the Miami riots of 1980, I have to wonder if nothing became of my case because of pressure from 'higher up' in the legal system, to quietly kick the whole thing into the long grass, or at least ignore it until it faded away. It would be understandable that the state authorities would want to avoid any potential situation that might inflame a new round of riots and violence, considering that the events of that May led to at least eighteen deaths and over $100 million worth of property damage.

Perhaps my long search to find justice and a 'marker' fell foul of that need to keep the peace, in which case I fell victim a second time. This time, in the broadest sense, to political concerns.

I was led down the civil route to justice, so I now wanted an expert eye cast over our civil case, and in particular over what I thought was the hub of our failure in 1987; the choice of target in the lawsuits. Our two lawyers chose the Dollar franchisee at Miami airport, notwithstanding that the company had filed for bankruptcy two years before. I questioned that at the time and spoke to the British Franchise Association, who advised that we added to the lawsuit the very viable Dollar franchisor in California; advice rejected by my legal advisor at the time, and very vociferously by my lawyers a couple of years later. My legal advisor still sticks to his guns, saying just recently, 'There was no principle in law (either in the UK or the USA) that a parent company can be held responsible for the acts of the subsidiary company, because they are separate legal entities.' In this confident sentence Alistair rejected my claim of the last thirty-eight years, but was he right?

I don't think he was. I went to the very top, and spent time with John Pratt, senior partner of Hamilton Pratt, and a past Chair of the International Bar Association's International Franchise Committee and Director of the American Bar Association's International Franchising Division. As if that wasn't enough, by way of credentials, John is author of *Franchising: Law and Practice*, and to top it all, he is rated by *Who's Who Legal* as Europe's leading franchise lawyer. I couldn't wish for anyone more informed.

John said my legal advisor was 'confused'. The relationship between the two 'Dollars' was not that of parent and subsidiary; it was franchisor/franchisee. It made sense to include the Dollar franchisor on those lawsuits unless there was a very obvious reason not to do so.

John had skimmed through the Avis v O'Boyle case quoted to me in 1983 which showed the merit of including the franchisor, and he agreed that to do so followed a well-worn path. It made sense, he said, to include the franchisor if I was going to criticise the training of the rental agents and their understanding of the term 'fully insured' as it relates to a foreign visitor. And if I was to criticise the contract I was given for not offering appropriate insurance.

The second big reason for including the franchisor is that they usually have deeper pockets… which was very pertinent in my case where the franchisee was already bankrupt.

I showed John my rebuttal of Lawyer S's argument as to the inclusion of the franchisor. He confirmed that there *was* a possible direct management involvement from the franchisor because they produced a uniform contract, a copy of which their franchisees would have given me. It *was* the franchisor who had waived the cover I needed, and who set the standards for the training of staff which could have included knowledge of the differences in European insurance systems.

The case would have had to be proven, but I left John's office vindicated and angry. The franchisor's name should have been on those lawsuits and all three of my lawyers had been funda-mentally wrong to ignore my concern.

To have won the lawsuit, or to have had a proper investiga-tion and prosecution, would not have brought my family back. And it's too late to persuade Mr Anderson not to ignore those blazing headlights bearing down on him on that otherwise dark night in the Everglades.

But my family deserved more than the deafening silence that followed a tragic night in February 1981. I met but wasn't heard by people who mattered. Including Members of Parliament, District Attorneys, and the Florida State Attorney.

Did I really need an army of television cameras and expensive lawyers behind me to persuade the Miami police to lift the shutters that were slammed shut after I left their shores?

Is a high profile and money generating civil suit the only way to justice in the USA?

Or

does the 'Land of the Free' look after its own, leaving the proverbial devil to take the hindmost?

Everything went fatally wrong on 17 February 1981. But with the completion of this book, and as a massive chapter of my life slips into the past, the very best of times will stay with me.

Adrienne, Nigel, Anna-Jane and Lucy-Claire.
Always innocent and forever beautiful.

THE END